First World War
and Army of Occupation
War Diary
France, Belgium and Germany

37 DIVISION
63 Infantry Brigade,
Brigade Machine Gun Company
1 August 1916 - 28 February 1918

WO95/2529/4

The Naval & Military Press Ltd
www.nmarchive.com
Published in association with The National Archives

Published by

The Naval & Military Press Ltd

Unit 10 Ridgewood Industrial Park,

Uckfield, East Sussex,

TN22 5QE England

Tel: +44 (0) 1825 749494

www.naval-military-press.com

www.nmarchive.com

This diary has been reprinted in facsimile from the original. Any imperfections are inevitably reproduced and the quality may fall short of modern type and cartographic standards.

© Crown Copyright
Images reproduced by permission of The National Archives, London, England, 2015.

Contents

Document type	Place/Title	Date From	Date To
Heading	WO95/2529/4		
Heading	Reference WO95 2529 63rd Machine Gun Coy. Aug 1916-Feb 1918 Conservation Department		
Heading	37th Division 63rd Infy Bde 63rd Machine Gun Coy. Aug 1916-Feb 1918. From 21 Div 63 Bde.		
Miscellaneous	O.L. 63 Machine Gun Coy D.A.G. 31 Echelon.		
War Diary	Cabaret Rouge Advanced Company For Berthonval Sector	01/08/1916	11/08/1916
War Diary	Chateau de La Haie	12/08/1916	14/08/1916
Heading	Dieval	15/08/1916	15/08/1916
War Diary	Cabblain L'Abbe	23/08/1916	01/09/1916
War Diary	Fresvillers	02/09/1916	14/09/1916
War Diary	Grand	15/09/1916	15/09/1916
War Diary	Servins	16/09/1916	17/09/1916
Heading	Aix Noulette	18/09/1916	18/09/1916
Miscellaneous	D.C. 63 Machine Gun Coy. 37th Division. Memorandum.		
War Diary	Souchez	01/10/1916	15/10/1916
War Diary	Fresnicourt	16/10/1916	17/10/1916
War Diary	Fresvillers	18/10/1916	19/10/1916
War Diary	Liencourt	20/10/1916	21/10/1916
War Diary	Orville	21/10/1916	21/10/1916
War Diary	Terramesnil	22/10/1916	31/10/1916
Heading	A Form. Messages And Signals.		
War Diary	Terramesnil	01/11/1916	01/11/1916
War Diary	Beauval	02/11/1916	07/11/1916
War Diary	Lucheux	08/11/1916	11/11/1916
War Diary	Lealvillers	13/11/1916	13/11/1916
War Diary	Hedauville	14/11/1916	14/11/1916
War Diary	Beaucourt	20/11/1916	30/11/1916
War Diary	Raincheval	01/12/1916	09/12/1916
War Diary	Terramesnil	14/12/1916	14/12/1916
War Diary	Remaisnil	15/11/1916	15/11/1916
War Diary	Boubers Antin	16/12/1916	16/12/1916
War Diary	Fontaines	17/12/1916	17/12/1916
War Diary	Busnes	18/12/1916	21/12/1916
War Diary	Busnes La Tombe Willot	22/12/1916	31/12/1916
Heading	War Diary B3 N. G Coy. Vol XI		
Heading	Headquarters 37th Division Herewith War Diary For January 1917. Please Acknowledge receipt		
War Diary	Veille Chapelle	01/01/1917	03/01/1917
War Diary	Neuve Chapelle	03/01/1917	31/01/1917
Heading	War Diary 63rd M.G. Coy Feb 1917 Vol 12		
War Diary	Ferme du Bois	01/02/1917	02/02/1917
War Diary	Beuvry	02/02/1917	11/02/1917
War Diary	Les Brebis	12/02/1917	12/02/1917
War Diary	Loos Salient	12/02/1917	28/02/1917
Miscellaneous	O C 63re M.G. Coy 39th Division Memorandum.	31/03/1917	31/03/1917
War Diary	Les Brebis	28/02/1917	28/02/1917
War Diary	La Bourse	01/03/1917	03/03/1917

War Diary	Lespesses	04/03/1917	09/03/1917
War Diary	Valhuon	09/03/1917	09/03/1917
War Diary	Gouy En Ternois	10/03/1917	17/03/1917
War Diary	Gouy	18/03/1917	31/03/1917
War Diary	Gouy		
Miscellaneous	O.C. 63. M.G. Coy.		
War Diary	Gouy-En. Ternois.	05/03/1917	09/03/1917
War Diary	Arras		
War Diary	Arras	13/03/1917	13/03/1917
War Diary	Duisans	14/03/1917	14/03/1917
War Diary	Agnes Duisans	15/03/1917	16/03/1917
War Diary	Montenescourt	19/03/1917	27/03/1917
War Diary	Manin	01/05/1917	01/05/1917
War Diary	Simencourt.	18/05/1917	18/05/1917
War Diary	Dainville	19/05/1917	19/05/1917
War Diary	Arras	21/05/1917	28/05/1917
War Diary	Tilloy	29/05/1917	30/05/1917
War Diary	Arras	31/05/1917	31/05/1917
Heading	War Diary 63rd M.G. Coy June 1917 Vol 16		
Miscellaneous	A Form. Messages And Signals.		
War Diary	Arras	01/06/1917	01/06/1917
War Diary	Manin	02/06/1917	09/06/1917
War Diary	Hezecques	10/06/1917	10/06/1917
War Diary	Rely	22/06/1917	22/06/1917
War Diary	Steenbecque	23/06/1917	23/06/1917
War Diary	St. Silvestre Cappel	24/06/1917	24/06/1917
War Diary	Klondyke Farm	25/06/1917	29/06/1917
War Diary	In The Line	30/06/1917	30/06/1917
Heading	War Diary 63 Machine Gun Co/II July 1917 Vol 17		
War Diary		01/07/1917	03/07/1917
War Diary	Donegal Farm	04/07/1917	15/07/1917
War Diary	In Line	16/07/1917	20/07/1917
War Diary	Donegal Farm	21/07/1917	29/07/1917
War Diary	In Line	30/07/1917	30/07/1917
Heading	War Diary 63rd M.G. Coy Aug 1917 Vol 18		
War Diary	In The Line	30/07/1917	02/08/1917
War Diary	In Line	03/08/1917	03/08/1917
War Diary	Bully Beef Farm	04/08/1917	04/08/1917
War Diary	Locrehof Farm	07/08/1917	08/08/1917
War Diary	La Polka Farm	09/08/1917	26/08/1917
War Diary	M. 21. B. 5.3	27/08/1917	28/08/1917
War Diary	In The Line	29/08/1917	31/08/1917
Heading	War Diary 63rd M.G. Coy. Sept 1917 Vol 19		
War Diary	In The Line Hollebeke Sector.	01/09/1917	06/09/1917
War Diary	In The Line	06/09/1917	06/09/1917
War Diary	N. 10.c.	07/09/1917	09/09/1917
War Diary	M 13 B.9.9	10/09/1917	13/09/1917
War Diary	M. 10 B 9.9	14/09/1917	17/09/1917
War Diary	M. 13.b.8.9	18/09/1917	18/09/1917
War Diary	Sheet 28 S.W. N.19.d.	19/09/1917	19/09/1917
War Diary	N.19.d. Central	20/09/1917	21/09/1917
War Diary	M.13.b.8.9	22/09/1917	28/09/1917
War Diary	I 30a 8815	29/09/1917	30/09/1917
Miscellaneous	63rd M.G. Coy. Fining Report Appendix A.		
Miscellaneous	63 M. Gun Coy Appendix B	01/10/1917	01/10/1917
Miscellaneous	67th Division Q	01/11/1917	01/11/1917

Heading	War Diary 63rd M.G. Coy. Oct 1917 Vol 20		
War Diary	Mount Sorrel I 30 C 95.90	01/10/1917	06/10/1917
War Diary	Beaver Camp N 15 C 34 Sheet 28 S.W.	07/10/1917	11/10/1917
War Diary	Edge Street Tunnels	12/10/1917	12/10/1917
War Diary	Mount Sorrel	13/10/1917	16/10/1917
War Diary	Frontier Camp M 7 0.8.2. France 28 S.W.	17/10/1917	17/10/1917
War Diary	Frontier Camp	18/10/1917	20/10/1917
War Diary	Merris	21/10/1917	31/10/1917
Map	63rd Inf. Bde Section		
Map	Shrewsbury Forest		
Map	Message Map		
Miscellaneous	Message Form.		
Heading	Firing Reports. Appendix I		
Miscellaneous	63rd Machine Gun Coy Firing Report		
Miscellaneous	63rd Machine Gun Coy Firing Report	06/10/1917	06/10/1917
Miscellaneous	63rd Machine Gun Coy Firing Report		
Miscellaneous	Section Officer No 4 Section 63rd M.G. Coy.	05/10/1917	05/10/1917
Miscellaneous	Section Officer No 4 Section 63rd M.G. Coy.	06/10/1917	06/10/1917
Miscellaneous	Total No Of Rounds Fired During The Month Of October		
Heading	Appendix No II Relief Orders		
Miscellaneous	63rd Machine Gun Company	06/10/1917	06/10/1917
Operation(al) Order(s)	63rd Infantry Brigade Order No. 171	13/10/1917	13/10/1917
Operation(al) Order(s)	63rd Infantry Brigade No. 2906 To All Recipients of Brigade order No. 171	13/10/1917	13/10/1917
Operation(al) Order(s)	63rd Infantry Brigade No. 29191 Amendment No. 2 To 63rd Inf. Bde. Order No. 171 Dated 13.10.17	13/10/1917	13/10/1917
Heading	Appendix No 3 Map		
Heading	Appendix IV Training Programme From 24-10-17 To 31-10-17		
Miscellaneous	Programme of Training 21.10.17 to 27.10.17	21/10/1917	21/10/1917
Miscellaneous	Programme Of Work 21.10.17 to 27.10.17	21/10/1917	21/10/1917
Miscellaneous	Programme of Training From 29.10.17 to 3.11.17	29/10/1917	29/10/1917
Miscellaneous	To H.Q. 37th Divn	01/11/1917	01/11/1917
War Diary	Merris	01/11/1917	10/11/1917
War Diary	N.10.a Adv Coy H.Q.	11/11/1917	11/11/1917
War Diary	Spoil Bank I 33.d.40.60. Rear H.Q Essex Camp N 21.a.1.9	12/11/1917	30/11/1917
Miscellaneous	Programme of Training 29.10.17 to 3.11.17 Appendix 1	29/10/1917	29/10/1917
Miscellaneous	Details of Gun Positions.	13/11/1917	13/11/1917
War Diary	Line	01/12/1917	29/12/1917
Heading	63rd Brigade. 37th Division. 63rd Machine Gun Company. January 1918		
Miscellaneous	Firing Report 63rd M.G. Coy	01/01/1918	01/01/1918
Miscellaneous	Firing Report 63rd M.G. Coy	02/01/1918	02/01/1918
Miscellaneous	Firing Report 63rd M.G. Coy	03/01/1918	03/01/1918
Miscellaneous	Firing Report 63rd M.G. Coy.	04/01/1918	04/01/1918
Miscellaneous	Firing Report 63rd M.G. Coy	05/01/1918	05/01/1918
Miscellaneous	Firing Report 63rd M.G. Coy	06/01/1918	06/01/1918
Miscellaneous	Firing Report 63rd M.G. Coy	07/01/1918	07/01/1918
Miscellaneous	Firing Report 63rd M.G. Coy	08/01/1918	08/01/1918
Miscellaneous	Firing Report 63rd M.G. Coy.	09/01/1918	09/01/1918
Miscellaneous	Firing Report 63rd M.G. Coy.	10/01/1918	10/01/1918
Miscellaneous	Firing Report 63rd M.G. Coy.	11/01/1918	11/01/1918
War Diary	Line	01/01/1918	11/01/1918
War Diary	T 27 Sheet 27. S.W.	12/01/1918	23/01/1918

War Diary	U.20.A.	24/01/1918	31/01/1918
Miscellaneous	Programme of Work 21/1/18-26/1/18	21/01/1918	21/01/1918
Miscellaneous	Programme Of Work		
Miscellaneous	Programme Of Work For Week Ending February 2nd 1918	02/02/1918	02/02/1918
Heading	63rd Brigade. 37th Division. Became Part of 37th Battalion M.G.C. in March. 63rd Machine Gun Company. February 1918		
War Diary	U 21a Sheet 27 S.W.	01/02/1918	13/02/1918
War Diary	Line	14/02/1918	28/02/1918
Miscellaneous	Programme Of Work For Week Ending February 2nd 1918 Appendix No 1	02/02/1918	02/02/1918
Miscellaneous	Programme Of Work For Week Ending February Appendix 2		
Miscellaneous	Programme Of Work For Week Ending February 16th 1918 Appendix 3	16/02/1918	16/02/1918
Miscellaneous	Firing Report	16/02/1918	16/02/1918
Miscellaneous	Firing Report	17/02/1918	17/02/1918
Miscellaneous	Firing Report	18/02/1918	18/02/1918
Miscellaneous	Firing Report	19/02/1918	19/02/1918
Miscellaneous	Firing Report	20/02/1918	20/02/1918
Miscellaneous	Firing Report	21/02/1918	21/02/1918
Miscellaneous	Firing Report	22/02/1918	22/02/1918
Miscellaneous	Firing Report	23/02/1918	23/02/1918
Miscellaneous	Firing Report	24/02/1918	24/02/1918
Miscellaneous	Firing Report	25/02/1918	25/02/1918
Miscellaneous	Firing Report	26/02/1918	26/02/1918
Miscellaneous	Firing Report	28/02/1918	28/02/1918

WO 95
2529/4

| REFERENCE | WO | 95 | 2529 | 63rd MACHINE GUN COY. AUG 1916 – FEB 1918 | CONSERVATION DEPARTMENT | |

37TH DIVISION
63RD INFY BDE

63RD MACHINE GUN COY.
AUG 1916 - FEB 1918.

From 21 DIV 63 BDE

Army Form C. 348.

MEMORANDUM.

From O.C. 63 Machine Gun Coy.

To D.A.G. 3/ Echelon.

August 31st 1916.

Herewith War Diary for the month of August - kindly acknowledge receipt.

W.J.A. Coldwell Major
(2/Northamptonshire (R))
O.C. 63 Machine Gun Coy.

WAR DIARY or ~~INTELLIGENCE SUMMARY~~

(Erase heading not required.)

Army Form C. 2118.

63 M.G. Coy

Place	Date	Hour	Summary of Events and Information	Remarks and references to Appendices
CABARET ROUGE. Advanced Company HQ for BERTHONVAL SECTOR	August 1st to 11th		Company in the trenches - Enemy's attitude quiet - this time was spent in opening up old trenches - constructing new M.G. Emplacements, reconstructing existing Emplacements and improving & constructing dug outs - A considerable amount of indirect fire was carried out on enemy trenches, dumps, roads etc - about 2000 rounds every other night being expended - Unfortunately the fact that the Enemy holds the crest of the VIMY RIDGE makes observation of his 2nd line trench system almost impossible - according to the map the ground to the E of this ridge falls away & could we establish ourselves actually on the very top of this ridge all his trench system would be exposed - On the 8th O.C. Coy went round the various gun emplacements with G.O.C. Brigade - The M Guns holding the ZOUAVE VALLEY should make this valley absolutely impossible to the Enemy - Unfortunately no R.E. labour was forthcoming & consequently no really shell proof dug outs could be constructed though it is true only a few were necessary. The Coy having taken over 70% deep dug outs to each gun position - The Enemy appears nervous opposite us - it is extremely probable that he	

WAR DIARY
or
INTELLIGENCE SUMMARY

63 M.G.Coy.

Army Form C. 2118
V6e 6

Place	Date	Hour	Summary of Events and Information	Remarks and references to Appendices
			a strongly fortifying his position for passive defence.	Unitiated
	12th	9.30am	O.C. 26th M.G. Coy. visits the two new posts, which all gun positions by 12 Coy. the (O.C. 21st C.oy) is to take. 63 M.G. Coy Barons 1/5 Inf. Bde. taken on 11M/12M August.	
CHATEAU DE LA HAIE	11th		63 M.G. Coy accordingly left Buecke and billets in CHATEAU DE LA HAIE - billets in Gardens - Co's paid and Remainder of the day devoted Fatigues, cleaning up kits etc.	
"	13th			
"	14th		Coy left billets at 7pm. Marched to DIEVAL - arriving 9pm - 15/8/16 - rations for coming - possibly early am. 63 rode ruled much extra in trucks.	
DIEVAL	15th		Coy paid and despatches having forwarded - Separate Rolls, For Rolls, retained via Telegrams ledgeman, Book mustering etc - also Range test - Tus Ing satisfactory. Coy carried on Extrade was held -	
	23rd			
CAMBLAIN L'ABBE	23rd	9pm	Coy marched 9pm to CAMBLAIN L'ABBE arriving at billets 6pm. Few stragglers	
	31st		Much personnel spent Camp out into much improved Mil fewer toasted. Nothing Extra-Rother foreign of the in Reserve of Brigade ett.	

WAR DIARY or ~~INTELLIGENCE SUMMARY~~

63 M.G. Coy

Army Form C. 2118.

Place	Date	Hour	Summary of Events and Information	Remarks and references to Appendices
Continued.			Much rain prevented the full training being carried out though half the Company was successfully put through practices on the range –	
	31st		Draft of 4 men arrived – this brings up the Company to full strength – they look smart men – have never been on service before –	

W.G.A. Coldwck Major
2/Northamptonshire Regt.
O.C. 63 Machine Gun Coy

Place	Date	Hour	Summary of Events and Information	Remarks and references to Appendices
CAMBLAIN L'ABBÉ	5th Sept		2 letters with list of names - No raid tonight -	
			32 other ranks (inc. 1 officer) midnight with celebration guide	
FRESVILLERS		9:10 a.m.	left billets to FRESVILLERS - dust track & some falling out - great	
			fatigue. Fine beautiful day	
"	3rd	6:15 p.m.	Nos 1 & 2 section marched off to SAINS. The attached to 189 Bngde for the line tonight.	
			Remainder Battn only on M.G. G2 - an extra tired out - the LORETTE RIDGE	
			was fairly or rather unnerving in detail	
		11¾	No 4 extra tired all round -	
			No 3 " afternoon } - All extended magazine to test, one front	
			from 25 [?] 250 yds - Sgts Btn Teaching Btn Ako Firearms -	
		5½	Rain & others - Interior Teapara Afters -	
		6/9	Ben Ali Belt - obtained for field aft - fellow in the Carpenter	
			of Carpenter (Mr) & highly [?] as it is [?] Ad the Tenne	
			but did all we can this the bad army men this [?] ([?])	
		7½	Eq founded in field - there had a certain amount ([?])	
		9½	As extended heavy fire - practice the Btt with trouble	

WAR DIARY or INTELLIGENCE SUMMARY.

63 M.G. Coy

Place	Date	Hour	Summary of Events and Information	Remarks and references to Appendices
FRESVILLERS			as for open fighting - this was combined with a route march - afternoon - Lecture on allocation of duties - Infantry Drill	
	9th		Limber Drill again carried out as for a Rear Guard action. Men armed with revolvers fired another course on the range - a small competition with prizes was also held - one has the satisfaction at all events of knowing that those armed with these weapons are more or less capable of handling them with less danger to others than formerly - 2 full range practices having been carried out & much revolver drill -	
	10th		Limber Drill as an advance guard - culminating in a line being held with M. Guns - cover, concealment, fields of fire being all taken into consideration, allowances being made for supposed breakdown of half limbers & mule casualties	
	11th		Range practices with particular attention to Stoppages all morning - A general improvement all round in gunnery noticed - Signalling class instituted	
	12th		Usual programme of work - with 1 hours Coy Drill under O.C. Coy carried out - a most important item sometimes forgotten in M.G. Coys - New standings for mule lines begun - Latrines improved - Washing bench made cutting up tables etc - the material having arrived last night -	

WAR DIARY
or
INTELLIGENCE SUMMARY.
(Erase heading not required.)

63 Inf. Bde.

Army Form C. 2118.

Place	Date	Hour	Summary of Events and Information	Remarks and references to Appendices
FRESNILLERS	13/5		Special army orders issued and handed to various Company officers — these orders contained plans for the attack — for us at all that is known — the Germans entrenched several advanced fiddle nests — this represents all we consider vulnerable, nor does the approach suffer.	
	14½		Brigade Moves to GRAND SERVINS at 15⁵⁰	
GRAND SERVINS	15/5	9.50 pm	A very useful th day passing carried out combined with good weather. Marched to GRAND SERVINS (15chm) Billets in suburb.	
SERVINS	16/5		Brigade H.qrs of Surk Agreem H.G. in CARENCY Sector. 14 June if 27th Inf.Gr.	
			4. BAROLE LINE — relief complete by midnight	
	17/5		9 am Orders for relief carried.	
			11 am Orders for Sork relieved 127th Inf Gr — relief complete 7.30 pm	
			12 Germans took over to AIX NOULETTE 6 xxxxx to — relief of Noord Brigade H.G. Gr.	
AIX NOULETTE	18/5		Brilliant Noord B.Hq Gr 2.3.4 xxxxxxx — relief complete 4.30 am. No 1 Bullion night rifle contact 11.30 pm — Aux kite over — 8 gun LORETTE RIDGE	
			N⁰ 5 — SOUCHEZ 1 on 4 2 — By xd trenches —	

WAR DIARY or INTELLIGENCE SUMMARY.

Army Form C. 2118

63 M.G. Coy

Place	Date	Hour	Summary of Events and Information	Remarks and references to Appendices
AIX NOULETTE			One section of 112 M.G. Coy attached to act as reserve.	
	19th		Gun positions satisfactorily arranged one gun altered - considerable amount of work to be done in the way of constructing dug outs and repairing trenches in	
	20th		the vicinity of M.G. emplacements - This work was begun at once & considerable	
	21st		progress being made - R.E. help being procured for construction of dug outs. No 3 section finds a dug out platoon of 19 men & 1 N.C.O. - Trenches not in any good state of repair and extremely wet - especially on LORETTE RIDGE - where much work is in progress i.e. duck boarding trenches -	
	22nd		2 guns (No 4 section) carried out 2 hours indirect night firing on enemy Transport Roads - usual work in progress	
	23rd		G.O.C. 37th Divn visited trenches with G.O.C. Brigade - O.C. M.G. Coy accompanying them - Indirect fire carried out for 2 hours by 2 guns No 1 section -	
	24th		Dug out platoon making good headway	
	25th		Indirect fire carried out 10.30 - 11.30 & 12 mn till 1 Am as on 23rd by No 1 section	
	26th		Trenches improving generally - weather being finer & much work being done everywhere - Enemy quiet - shows very little retaliation -	

WAR DIARY
or
INTELLIGENCE SUMMARY

63 M. G. Coy

(Erase heading not required.)

Army Form C. 2118.

Instructions regarding War Diaries and Intelligence Summaries are contained in F. S. Regs., Part II. and the Staff Manual respectively. Title pages will be prepared in manuscript.

Place	Date	Hour	Summary of Events and Information	Remarks and references to Appendices
AIX NOULETTE	27th		Throughout the night from 10 PM till 3 AM 5 guns kept up a constant fire upon the enemy transport roads behind their lines - also on enemy dumps etc - over 12000 rounds were fired - this was done in conjunction with Regimental Lewis guns - Enemy Mgnns retaliated upon the N. Slope of the LORETTE RIDGE - This was more or less an organised shoot -	
	28th 29th 30th		Usual Trench routine - with indirect fire from at least two guns on enemy roads dumps etc - During the last fortnight much good work has been done on the trenches & upon deep dug outs; the weather being very favourable for work - Horse standings improved also - On the 29th 1 Hotchkiss section attached to the Coy - this in addition to 1 section of the 112th M.G. Coy (thus giving a total Coy command of 24 guns) —	

W.G. A. Coldwell Major.
(2/Northamptonshire Regt)
O.C. 63 Machine Gun Coy

T.2134. Wt. W708—776. 50C000. 4/15. Sir J. C. & S.

Army Form C. 348.

MEMORANDUM.

From O.C. 63 Machine Gun Co. From

To 37th Division. To

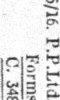

Oct 31st 1916.

Herewith War Diary of
63 Machine Gun Co –
for the month of October.

107. A. Colwill Major
(?) Northamptonshire R[?]
O.C. 63 Machine [Gun Co?]

ANSWER.

191 .

WAR DIARY or INTELLIGENCE SUMMARY

Army Form C. 2118.

63 M.G. Coy

Place	Date	Hour	Summary of Events and Information	Remarks and references to Appendices
SOUCHEZ	October 16	16"	Guns still in Trenches in SOUCHEZ & in LORETTE RIDGE – Enemy showed very considerable amount of Trench Mortar activity, does a fair deal of damage. Weather rather wet. The wind kept fairly cloudy and cleared away after night. With 2 L.G. guns, reasonably with 1 gun – kept in touch all case firing using single charged cord. –	
		At 10"	The Ridge hit our arches 500' of front du N. on gun commanded through to contact with Lieut Schroeder – His gun commanded a field position but to fire a further 60° behind our own field line – Very considerable amount of work carried out – 1 dug out archer if 18 in front – made in the R.E. dugout – 2 new deep dug out at large 15' deep (new shaft) 9 deep dug out made much fallen & considerably improved – many attacks this galley considered, broken pieces with duet trade – Nos 2 & 4 machine dugouts to the Nos 500' finish 9 –	
			duck Sunday it –	
		12"H	Hostile Shell of K.E.H. trenches but no activity on our part – 1 German plane brought down –	

WAR DIARY or ~~INTELLIGENCE SUMMARY.~~ 63. M.G. Coy

Army Form C. 2118.

Place	Date	Hour	Summary of Events and Information	Remarks and references to Appendices
SOUCHEZ	Oct. 15th		O.C. 6th Canadian M.G. Coy came over preparatory to relieving the Coy -	
FRESNICOURT	16th		Relief by above Coy. Coy relief complete by 2.30 PM. Sections rendez-vous at PETIT SAINS & marched to FRESNICOURT where Coy billeted	
	17th		Limbers repacked - Coy Hair cut - Underclothes etc issued out -	
FRESVILLERS	18th	10.15 AM	Coy marched to FRESVILLERS arriving at noon - billets taken over very dirty -	
	19th	11 AM	G.O.C's Conference at CHELERS - O.C. Coy attended -	
LIENCOURT	20th	8.45 AM	Coy marched with Brigade to LIENCOURT - good march - 6 stragglers - O.C. Coy went by bus with O.C's units in Brigade & G.O.C to ~~BETRAN~~ ENGLEBELMER to reconnoitre the line - preparatory for attack -	
" "	21st	9.13 AM	Coy marched with Brigade to ORVILLE where billets were found - excellent march only two stragglers - arrived in billets 2.45 PM	
ORVILLE			Left ORVILLE 10 AM arrived at TERRAMESNIL 22nd at 11 AM - billeted -	
TERRAMESNIL	22nd		Ordered to send 2/Lt Brazier away to 73 M.G. Coy - this in addition to an order requiring 2/Lt Tall to proceed to England (Grantham) - The Coy therefore depleted of two excellent officers within 2 days	

WAR DIARY
or
INTELLIGENCE SUMMARY

63 M.G.Coy

Army Form C. 2118.

Place	Date	Hour	Summary of Events and Information	Remarks and references to Appendices
TERRAMESNIL	22/7		Orders came for the Coy preparing to be flung into the scheme.	
			1/Lt Hance & Hurley were in town.	
	23rd		Asked W.O. for the authorities of 1 extra Q.M. Colour Sergt for M.G. Co. — the whole was the present considerable of the 2nd M.G. transport.	
			W. specialist Signallers	
	24th		2/Lt Rigg & Hurley joined the Company	
	25th		9/Lt Squitt joined the Coy. — 9/Lt Hayward posted as 9/O C. 63 M.G.B. Carlisle	
	26th		2/Lt Kerr took over troubles in the trenches at THIEPVAL, north of the ANCRE, in conjunction with the 152 Bde R.E. All details reconnoitred first.	
	6.		M. specialists take long intervals to work towards tier are carried out. Physical Training. Rest Parades. Lt/Lt Bell. Alexander & Kerr Joined with Geor Medium.	
	30th			
			H.E. & M.G. Dispose.	
	6.		Men took to own their canteen rations — so that up yesterday for Orderlies. It only confirm other in the Coy kept Coy busy.	
	31st		Coy wash, use Terracith, his Raymond.	
			Lt. A. Clark Hope (2/West Surrey Regt) OC 63 M.G. Carlisle

"A" Form.
MESSAGES AND SIGNALS.

TO: 39th Division.

Forward War diary of 630 Reserve
Gas Coy for the Month of November.

W.G.A. Coldwell Major
(Northamptonshire Regt)
O.C. 63 Machine Gun Coy

AAA

WAR DIARY
or
INTELLIGENCE SUMMARY

63. M.G.C.?

Army Form C. 2118.

Place	Date	Hour	Summary of Events and Information	Remarks and references to Appendices
	Nov. 1st			
TERRAMESNIL		10.30am	Gr paraded and moved to BEAUVAL, arriving in billets A.15.	
BEAUVAL	2nd	9.30	G.O.C inspected the Cr in fighting order - Kit test - afternoon, General clean up of Gun Kit. -	
	3rd	9. am	Cr Rad march 8 mile. -	
	4th	9.am	Rifle practice in attack, M. Guns taking up shoot points & beating off a barrage - attacked billets 2 P.m.	
	5th	10.30	Church Parade.	
	6th	9. a.m	Red horse to make contact with friendly Artillery patrols -	
		2.Pm	Billets & Trenches - Barrage practised -	
	7th			
LUCHEUX	8th	12.noon	Started for LUCHEUX via DOULLENS - arrived 3 Pm in billets	
	9th		Gr practised the advance, advancing over open country, taking up shoot points	
	10th	9.15 L.	Inse drill - Kit Inspection - 2 Pm Officers lecture - lecturing on shoot points for defence of a line (by Gen. O.C. cup). - Each officer & two staff officers attend lecture for instruction. - fatter after - cross fire - overhead fire for C.E.-	
	11th	8.15 Pm	Gr moved to LEAVILLERS, arriving 9 Pm (to shelter) billets. -	

WAR DIARY or INTELLIGENCE SUMMARY

63. M.G. Coy.

Army Form C. 2118.

(2)

Place	Date	Hour	Summary of Events and Information	Remarks and references to Appendices
LEALVILLERS	13th		Morning employed in thoroughly overhauling gun kit.	
HEDAUVILLE	14th	10 AM	Coy moved to HEDAUVILLE, bivouacked	
		7.PM	Coy left HEDAUVILLE & marched direct to trenches in the vicinity of BEAUCOURT (after the advance of the NAVAL DIVn, leaving transport close to ENGLEBELMER.	

Guns in position by 5.30 AM 15/11/16   8 guns being in the new front line around BEAUCOURT SUR ANCRE in the following positions (Ref 1:20,000 French map K.17 – M-21)

2 guns at R.7a.7.2.   2 guns at R.7b.1.3.   (No 1 section under 2/Lt Lenn)
2 guns at R.7d.8.9.   2 guns at R.7b.8.2.   (No 4 section under 2/Lt Crockatt).

Thus commanding the BOIS D'HOLLANDE RIDGE, PUISIEUX Rd RAVINE and the ANCRE VALLEY. One gun being layed on the Rd bridge R.8C.4.6.

Four guns (No 3 section) in immediate support in a trench running from about R.7C.2.7 to R.7C.6.3.

Four guns in reserve (No 2 section) at Q.12.d.6.1 in the Ravine.

This relief was effected by 5.30 AM under considerable hostile shelling & made more difficult by guides losing their way (which incidentally they never found again).

Throughout the next 3 days BEAUCOURT & its vicinity was heavily shelled by the Germans.

WAR DIARY
or
INTELLIGENCE SUMMARY. 63.M.G.Coy

Army Form C. 2118.

Place	Date	Hour	Summary of Events and Information	Remarks and references to Appendices

1/1 Lieut Roberts both being wounded, the position after 17th to the 15th - All our teams were exhausted & not until the difficult circumstances. Further few Explosions of under considerable shell fire -

On the evening of the 17th 2 Guns of No 2 section were sent into 8/S.L.I. also ANCRE T.B. that Regt in taking RIVER PUISIEUX T.B. with covering fire - These 2 Guns were found their Regt & dug in about R.8a.8.8. the same night -

From the night of May 15th up till the time the above of the 8/S.L.I. fire was kept up at the intervals by our troops (direct indirect) on flanks of R.8.C.4.6. - ANCRE VALLEY, and the

PUISIEUX R? RAVINE - The latter two length times fired on up till the 20th
On the morning of 18th a direct target presented itself in the form of about 100 German retiring in the PUISIEUX R? RAVINE, this was taken full advantage of by Rifleman (No. 1200)

Rifleman shot with —

On the afternoon of 18th at 2 pm 1 No 2 section at R.8a.8.8. fired direct targets in
PUISIEUX T.B. at 4- 8/S.L.1 advanced towards RIVER T.B.

On the night of 18th in ? 4/Middlesex Regt both ran fire. 8/S.L.1 - No 1 section fire used
to support them - No 1 section position at R.7f.1.3 fired take over by 2 Guns of No 3 section

WAR DIARY or INTELLIGENCE SUMMARY. 63. M.G. Coy

Army Form C. 2118.

(Erase heading not required.)

Place	Date	Hour	Summary of Events and Information	Remarks and references to Appendices
			No 1 Section took up its position in QUARRY at R.8.a.2.1. One gun being sent out in advance of the line each night up to the 20th as an advanced gun to prevent any surprise attack on the part of the Germans – Sgt Ryrie of this section doing particularly good work in encouraging his section, regardless of personal danger, & himself taking out the advanced gun on the night 19th/20th – About 3.30 PM the gun teams of No 2 section at R.8.a.8.8. were knocked out by shell fire with the exception of 1 L/Cpl & 2 men – Meanwhile 1 gun of No 4 section remained trained on the bridge at R.8.c.4.6. as a precautionary measure though it ceased fire owing to an advance on GRANDCOURT by troops S. of the river on the 18th – On the evening of the 20th the Coy was relieved – total casualties 4 officers 29 men – (14/15th to 20th) Throughout these operations, weather conditions were severe & hostile shelling considerable though comparatively little hostile sniping & M.G. fire – It is satisfactory to think that several direct targets were engaged with good results – R A T I O N S. Rations were brought up to Brigade dump by pack Transport, this method being very satisfactory –	

The enemy trenches in rather cramped parts - Just past our first line trench and up the hill, also to the right his trenches & tracks - Ten men also took to the funnel from by the water tower followed by three A.A.-

COMMUNICATION.
Communication between Co. HQ, Bn. HQs, the Arches was kept fairly good, there was 2 men for each Bn. and one G.H.Q. orderly -
Signals good but Bns kept below the ledger Hqn HQ as direct approaches to these Hqs and front line HQs all day by the Germans) FRICOURT Pn. July 1st & 2nd -

OBSERVATIONS.
a. Field transport by salvo for.
b. In my opinion the enemy stood the three days of Artillery preparation by Frederick cutting in places when batteries in reproduction to reinforcements & light fire (This is due by the Germans)
c. Prisoners when about to voice is there of food need. Thus being Enr. to eat especially of water. Like be supplied - and over the CSM to eat etc. -

WAR DIARY or INTELLIGENCE SUMMARY. 63. M.G. Coy

Place	Date	Hour	Summary of Events and Information	Remarks and references to Appendices
			d. Water carried in petrol tins is the only practical way of carrying up water -	
			e. 2 Shovels per gun team is absolutely necessary.	
			f. M.Guns can <u>not</u> keep up with infantry, when man handled except under the <u>most</u> favourable circumstances -	
			g. 8 belt boxes per gun should normally be a maximum amount to be carried forward belts can be refilled by the rifle ammunition on the man -	
			h. Great coats (in Winter) should be carried into the trenches & not sent up later -	
			i. Sufficient personnel be left with the Co's transport to attend to cooking of rations etc to be sent up to the line	
			j. The absence of a Cooker was much felt - It was impossible to borrow one from any Battalion as the only cooker not actually wanted by the 4/ Middlesex Regt was cooking food for German prisoners!	
			k. A thinner oil for M. Guns in cold weather is very necessary as the present oil congeals in cold weather	

WAR DIARY or INTELLIGENCE SUMMARY

63. M.G.Coy.

Army Form C. 2118.

Place	Date	Hour	Summary of Events and Information	Remarks and references to Appendices
BEAUCOURT	20.11	5pm	Coy in billets except No 3 section. – Coy withdrew to billets today and is in HAMEL – joined by No 3 section 3PM 21/11/16 in billets –	
	21st	6.230	Trench Kit spare pack mules up for a salvage dump, an unexpired builded Coy when as much as possible and cleared up their guns. Kit etc.	
	24th	8.15 AM	Coy marched to ENGLEBELMER B.T.W.E.	
	25th	11 AM	Coy marched to MAILLY-MAILLET B.T.W.E. – Very bad	
	26th	8.30 AM	Coy left MAILLY MAILLET and marched to RAINCHEVAL, via BETRANCOURT + LOUVENCOURT. It was marching extremely well – no straggles – Arrived RAINCHEVAL 12 noon – Billets –	
	27th		Having references checks & general, cleaning up – Equipment – guns – gun kit etc. during week – unpacking of kits –	
	28th		Cleaning up continued – 2i/c Coy inspection 2PM.	
	29th 9 to	6.11 AM	Coy tactics – Officers classes on trucking of intelligence at 2nd Staff joins the Coy	
	30th		Physical Training – Schools, Drill – etc	

Major A. Gotwell,
O.C. 63 Machine Gun Coy

WAR DIARY or INTELLIGENCE SUMMARY.

Army Form C. 2118.

63 Machine Gun Coy

Vol 10

Place	Date	Hour	Summary of Events and Information	Remarks and references to Appendices
RAINCHEVAL	Dec. 1st		Coy in billets at RAINCHEVAL.	
	2nd	8.30 AM	Coy moved to TERRAMESNIL to billets. The Coy billeted here till the 14th and during this period all articles required to complete establishment were indented for, ie harness gun equipment clothing etc. A programme of work was carried out on the following lines	

First Week:
- Physical Training 3 Hours
- Route Marching 7 "
- Mechanism & Stoppages 3 "
- Gun Drill 1 "
- Infantry Drill 3 "
- Officers scheme 2 "
- Field Training 2½ "
- Lectures to N.C.Os 2 "
- Range 2 "

2nd week:
- 3 Hours
- 6 "
- 2 "
- —
- 4 "
- 2 "
- 3 "
- 2 "
- 2 "

| | 9th | 9.15 AM | Corps Commander inspected the whole Brigade - in the notes by the Div'nl Commr issued subsequently the turn out of the Company was good. | |

WAR DIARY or INTELLIGENCE SUMMARY

63 Machine Gun Coy

Army Form C. 2118.

Place	Date	Hour	Summary of Events and Information	Remarks and references to Appendices
HAUTE-VISSE			via Ligne, MULEUX - DOULLENS - MEZEROLLES -	
TERRAMESNIL	14th	9.45	G⁹ motor with the Brigade to REMAISNIL, returns to Lillet 3.30 PM - no shoots	
REMAISNIL	15th	11 AM	Motor to BOUBERS via FROHEN-LE-GRAND - VILLERS L'HOPITAL - FORTEL and VACQUERIE, la chaffeur arrived in Lillet 2 PM	
BOUBERS	16th	9.15 AM	Motor to ANTIN, via NUNCQ ST POL - arrived in Lillet 3 PM - no shoots -	
ANTIN			Motor to FONTAINES LES HERMAIS via TANGRY - FIEFS - NEDONCHELLE, arrived in Lillet 2 PM - no shoots -	
FONTAINES	17th	10 AM	Motor to S.W. end of BUSNES LE FIRE, arrived in Lillet 2.30 PM - 1 shoot	
BUSNES	18th		Great clean up of guns. Equipped testers etc -	
"	19th			
"	20th		G⁹ talked to BUSNES, excellent talks, tried no understanding -	
"	21st			
BUSNES	22nd	9.30	G⁹ Practice march with the Brigade to Lillet at LA TOMBE WILLOT via main line N of LOCON	
LA TOMBE WILLOT			no shoots - in Lillet by 2.45 PM - fair little feed hampered have -	
	23rd		Usual training programme -	
	24th		Rest hands of Wills - Great in the trenches (very successful)	
	25th		Mess Buz. B⁴ G⁹ Walker takes departure, his late G.O.C. 87th Bn.²⁸	

WAR DIARY or INTELLIGENCE SUMMARY.

63 M.G. Coy

Army Form C. 2118.

Place	Date	Hour	Summary of Events and Information	Remarks and references to Appendices
"	"		This line is well sighted & in fairly good repair - Concrete M.G. Emplacements - these would not keep out a 4.2 How: shell and are rather too conspicuous - It might have been better policy to construct good M.G. dug outs with open Emplacements, or Emplacements made simply splinter & weather proof - Xmas day spent very quietly - no cases of Drunkenness.	
"	26th	9am	Physical training & Rout march to work off any effects of Xmas festivities.	
	27th 28th 29th 30th		Usual training exercises carried out - including a good deal of bombing practice & a bombing competition - certain portions of the Corps line visited in combination with a Rout march - 37th Div'al trench orders thoroughly explained to all ranks. - 29th & 30th O.C. Coy visited Village line with G.C. 63rd Bde, this line is in a bad state -	
	30th		O.C. Coy & 4 section officers visited the new line to be taken over i.e. from NEUVE CHAPELLE to about 1500x South - all details for relief arranged - Amongst other things O.C. Coy visited the old British front line left on March 10th 1915. -	
	31st	11am	Coy moved to new billets in VIEILLE CHAPELLE.	

W.G.A. Coldwell Major
(2/Northamptonshire R⁺)
O.C. 63 M.G. Coy

WAR DIARY

65/1 F Gp

IX 2⁰ B

To.

Headquarters
37th Division.

Herewith War Diary for
January 1917.
Please acknowledge receipt.

T Charles Watson Lt. O.C.
63rd Company.
Machine Gun Corps.

1st February 1917

WAR DIARY
or INTELLIGENCE SUMMARY

63 Machine Gun Coy

Army Form C. 2118.

Place	Date	Hour	Summary of Events and Information	Remarks and references to Appendices
VEILLE CHAPELLE	January 1917 1st		Company training - Section of men absorbing fire -	
	2nd		One Gun team section absorbed the 1st of No III Coy in the NEUVE CHAPELLE Subsection	
NEUVE CHAPELLE	3rd		Coy relieved III[?] MG Coy in the NEUVE CHAPELLE Section - 13 guns fire in the line w/ 3 SA 1:40,009. 3 in reserve at Coy HQ. R.36.d.65.15. Relief complete by 2.15 pm - Barnyard and Qr hr. blow unaimed of VEILLE CHAPELLE. Gun positions were not well placed, the angles being fixed facing a series of gaps in the front line - all the fire being frontal - guns varying from 200° to 300°. Behind the gaps and openings four of which are a relief from the infantry, stood the ready rifle gun - all fire supplementing open objectives to cover from the front rifle, Mh gun, which at this time was of the fire importance - To prevent at all times work for our second line of defence - is the 3 fire according during the first 6 days given are indubitable datings - No guns fire placed in the front line and 3 guns well forward the fire independent lights indoor to rear on 'line' placed in position with overhead cover, others, the immediate fire on 'line' placed in position with overhead cover, others, were in some cases double than for the tangle there in front of it for and	6 69

and the [?] of NEUVE CHAPELLE -

WAR DIARY or INTELLIGENCE SUMMARY

Army Form C. 2118.

63. M.G. Coy

Place	Date	Hour	Summary of Events and Information	Remarks and references to Appendices
	to 6th		NEUVE CHAPELLE, covered emplacements with open alternative ones being either found or constructed – dug outs in some cases being made for the teams – though these of course were of the Bairnsfather type (though superior to those of 1914) – deep dug outs, as in the country further South being impossible owing to the nature of the Country – A considerable amount of work being done, in some cases walls being removed to admit a better field of fire. Little night firing was carried out during this period as Gun teams were too busy – the reserve section supplying working parties to help in the work.	
	7th		Guns all in their new positions	
	8th		Indirect fire carried out on to the LA TOURELLE X ROADS & the Distillery behind from 11.30 PM to 4 AM at intervals – work continued on new positions & on horse standings –	
	9th		Indirect fire carried out from 11 PM to 12.30 AM on the BOIS DU BIEZ – 3 guns.	
	10th		In combination with the French mortars & artillery (firing from 7 AM to 9 AM) 3 Vickers guns kept up a practically continuous fire from 7 AM to 4.30 PM on the BOIS DU BIEZ firing about 6,000 rounds – Enemy retaliation was not very great though COPSE STREET was blown in in 3 places	

WAR DIARY
or
INTELLIGENCE SUMMARY.
(Erase heading not required.)

Army Form C. 2118.

63. Machine Gun Co⁴

Instructions regarding War Diaries and Intelligence Summaries are contained in F. S. Regs., Part II. and the Staff Manual respectively. Title pages will be prepared in manuscript.

Place	Date	Hour	Summary of Events and Information	Remarks and references to Appendices
	10th		Indirect fire carried out from 11 pm to 12.30 pm (one gun) along the S.W edge of the	
	11th		BOIS DU BIEZ, LIGNY LE PETIT, & Fᵐᵉ DU BIEZ.	
	12ᵗ		G.O.C. Brigade visited gun positions with O.C Co⁴	
	13ᵗ		About 10.000 rounds fired. direct & indirect, no immediate retaliation except an	
	14ᵗ		increase in enemy MG fire & a certain amount of searching for our M guns with shell fire	
	15ᵗ		O.C. Co⁴ visited A⁴ Army workshop, particularly to see an anti aircraft mounting —	
			the mounting is of a most satisfactory type —	
	16ᵗ		111 M.G. Co⁴ took over from 63 M.G. Co⁴ relief complete by 2PM - Co⁴ marched back to	
			billets at VEILLE CHAPELLE	
	17ᵗ		Co⁴ employed constructing horse standings & doing the usual training with the gun,	
			rout marching - 3 days range practice- revolver drill & shooting. G.O.C 37ᵗ Di⁴ inspected	
			the Co⁴ on the 22ⁿᵈ, followed up by inspection of G.O.C Brigade on the 26ᵗ —	
			26ᵗ O.C. Co⁴ visited new line to be taken over on 29ᵗ	
			27ᵗ Co⁴ bathed at LOCON.	
	28ᵗ		Sections at disposal of section officers to prepare for the taking over of trenches	
			nature of the line explained etc —	

T2134. Wt. W708 —776. 50000. 4/15. Sir J. C. & S.

WAR DIARY or INTELLIGENCE SUMMARY

63. M.G. Coy

Place	Date	Hour	Summary of Events and Information	Remarks and references to Appendices
	29th		Coy relieved 112 M.G. Coy in the FERME DU BOIS section - relief complete by 2 PM.	
	30th		Indirect fire carried out from 6 PM to 10.30 PM on back areas & approaches. A German relief being expected.	
	31st		Preparations for Indirect fire made (6 guns) in conjunction with an Inf'y raid by 111 Bde - Cancelled 3 PM - Relief orders issued for Feb 1st - Coy move out of the line.	

W.G.A. Coldwell Major
(2/Northamptonshire R.)
O.C. 63 Machine Gun Coy

WAR DIARY
63rd M.G. Coy
1st 1917

WAR DIARY OF INTELLIGENCE SUMMARY

63rd Machine Gun Company

Army Form C. 2118.

Place	Date	Hour	Summary of Events and Information	Remarks and references to Appendices
FERME DU BOIS	1.2.17		Company in the trenches. Orders for relief of the Coy by 15th M.G. Coy, 15th Inf. Bde. received.	
"	2.2.17		Guides from gun teams met the new company at 11 A.M. Relief complete by 3 p.m. Company marched by sections to BEUVRY. The whole division to which Coy. was attached was now in G.H.Q. reserve.	
BEUVRY	3.2.17		All gun kit & equipment cleaned. Spare kit dumped at BETHUNE. Company under orders to move at 8 hrs notice.	
"	4.2.17		Church parades. Repacking of limbers ready for move. Programme of training for the week ending Sat. 10th Feb. forwarded to 63rd Inf. Bde.	
"	5.2.17		Physical Training, Gun Drill, Infantry Drill, Revolver Drill & practices. Lecture on "Discipline".	
"	6.2.17		Training continued. Route March (6 miles) with 1st Line Transport. Practice in entraining & detraining carried out.	
"	7.2.17		Training as on the 5th inst. Respirator Drill. Range practices for two sections.	
"	8.2.17		Physical Training, gun drill, Lectures on "Sanitation" & "Range Cards". Two sections on the range. Orders received that the 37th Division would relieve the 24th Division in the hrs. Bois & Hallut sector. Preliminary reconnaissance carried out.	
"	9.2.17		Physical training, gun drill, infantry drill, revolver practice, inspection of guns, gun kit, of men's kit & equipment.	

WAR DIARY
or
INTELLIGENCE SUMMARY

(Erase heading not required.)

63rd Machine Gun Company

Army Form C. 2118.

Place	Date	Hour	Summary of Events and Information	Remarks and references to Appendices
BEUVRY	10.2.17		Route March (Guide) Salmu is Bas Bor Hazebrouk offered to attach to us for marching	
"	11.2.17		Orders posted ready for relief of 187 Machine Gun Company Reconnaissance by Section Officers of the village & RESERVE LINE in Mr. Morris Section Church Road.	
LES AREBIS	12.2.17		Company moved off from BEUVRY at 10.30 a.m., arriving at LES AREBIS at 12.25 p.m.	
		5pm	Co marched up the line, relieving 187 M.G Co - relief complete 9 PM -	
LOOS SALIENT			Had pack in the trenches making things in general for men comfortable - Bed Cutter 1 deep - During this period in the trenches my particular attention was paid to keep things - to gain their use up in the RESERVE LINE - 300° to 800° Relief in pid divert - to give is rising fire - 2 in centre of Co. H.Q. -	
	27/2		Had from trench dug dry up, with the School supplementers - (a that Supplementers wonderful for confidence & the men in case of a heavy bombardment - this avertium came in practice a man was... of dust... Many to men not reliable to safer, the moral effect is good) Over 50,000 bombs were found between the 13th & 27th feb by day (47th Corps) by night - No fires were carried out in a heavy... manner plus rifle at... there fired a explainable barrage the night	

WAR DIARY or INTELLIGENCE SUMMARY.

Army Form C. 2118.

63 M.G. Coy

Place	Date	Hour	Summary of Events and Information	Remarks and references to Appendices
Continued			also enemy dumps - new works in progress - Battⁿ H.Q. ek - gaps in enemy wire were fired on in long bursts every 5 minutes on the nights of 25th 26th 27th from stand to in the evening to stand to in the morning - this drew considerable enemy M.G. retaliation - In some cases enemy MGs were engaged by our M.Gs as their guns can be plainly seen at night, from the top of the CRASSIER. - Work Done - many open arm chair emplacements converted to the Y emplacement (i.e. with a trench running round the right side of the emplacement to enable N° 2 to attend to the gun properly - trenches cleared - existing covered emplacements improved - loopholes re screened - quick release gun brackets put up in shafts of deep dug outs - ek -	
	27th	10.P.M.	The 63rd Inf^t Brigade carried out a Dummy Raid on the German trenches in front of Puits 14 Bis - a considerable amount of retaliation was drawn from the enemy in the way of both field guns, M.Gs & Trench mortars - 14 guns of this Company cooperated together with this raid also 16 guns of the M.G. Co^y on the right & left - over 70,000 rounds in all being fired - It is hoped with good result -	
	28th		Co^y relieved by 18th M.G. Co^y	

W. A. Coldwell Major
(2/Northamptonshire R^t)
O.C. 63 Machine Gun Co^y

Army Form C. 348.

MEMORANDUM.

From O C 63rd 4" 9 Coy

To 37TH Division

31/3/17 1917.

Herewith War Diary of above Unit for month of March.

W.A. Coldwell Major
OC 63 H.y 6 y

WAR DIARY or INTELLIGENCE SUMMARY

Army Form C. 2118.

Vol 13

63. Machine Gun Coy.

Place	Date	Hour	Summary of Events and Information	Remarks and references to Appendices
LES BREBIS.	28th Feb.		Coy relieved in the LOOS salient by 18th M.G. Coy - marched direct to LA BOURSE (less 2 gun teams No 4 section) - arriving in billets at 3. A.M.	
LA BOURSE.	1st & 2nd		Coy remained in billets here till the morning of the 3rd when we marched to	
	3rd	9.30.?	ROBECQ billeting there for the night -	
LESPESSES.	4th to 9th	9.30 am	We moved to LESPESSES where we remained till the 9th, training being carried out - Infantry Drill - Gun Drill Etc -	
VALHUON	9th	8.40 AM	We moved with the Brigade direct to VALHUON - snow fell -	
GOUY EN TERNOIS	10th	8.40 am	We moved with the Brigade direct to GOUY EN TERNOIS - Orders received that this would be our training area -	
	11th		Sunday -	
	12th to 14th		Beginning of training period - training hours normally 8.30 AM to 12.30 PM and 2PM to 4 PM - the following points were specially attended to Gun Drill - Infantry Drill - Revolver practice & drill - judging distance officers & N.C.O's scheme - Ranges - Range competition won by No 3 section - Route marches (2 during the week) Lectures - M.Gs in advance methods of advancing through barrage fire also practical demonstration - Lectures Esperit de corps - discipline - Essays on discipline written by all ranks	

Place	Date	Hour	Summary of Events and Information	Remarks and references to Appendices
GOUY	18	8½	Physical Training - during given in ample dose - Bombing Instruction - telephones - N.C.O's drill etc.-	
		18½	Tour 18th 9th. The Companies were able to billets - training of a welter nor advanced character was carried out, Either comprising certain etc.- A great deal of attention has been paid to the Lewis gun specialised Lewis gunner N.C.O classes being found daily in this subject by the 82. Company- and evening - special attention being given to the care of the grains. E of ARRAS-	
		7	Changes from Winter trench trace to mobilisation were practised with considerable success.- The Company Pioneers took over much in evidence - and recent battles (viz. Catterall / Sudden) were played off - N 2 sector-	
		25½	Lectures Viverey- 3 Officers visited ARRAS the Battle fields End 1st 2nd for Intense training.-	
			Pioneers carried has 3 & 4 days -

WAR DIARY
(Intelligence Summary struck through)

63 M.G. Coy

Army Form C. 2118.

Place	Date	Hour	Summary of Events and Information	Remarks and references to Appendices
GOUY	26th to 31st		Another weeks training carried out - 1 Route march in which Limber, pack & manhandle transport was carried out. - Sections in open order in the advance - use of existing cover, & improvement of that cover practiced - Infantry drill - action from pack mules & from limbers. - Coy in the attack - 2 sections putting up Indirect fire barrage to assist Infantry advance, direction elevation etc being worked out by N.C.Os. - 2 sections advancing to consolidate captured position. Range cards & judging distance - N.C.O's Indirect fire class - all forming the basis of the weeks programme. - In the afternoon of the 29th 111th Infy Bde Assault at Arms - Several events open to the Division - of these events the 63rd M.G. Coy won the M.G. Competition - action from limbers - time taken galloping 100x into action - running 50x & getting into action 70 seconds - 72 seconds getting out of action -	

WAR DIARY
or
INTELLIGENCE SUMMARY

63 M.G.C.

Army Form C. 2118.

Place	Date	Hour	Summary of Events and Information	Remarks and references to Appendices
			The Brigade has taken tring just under 3 minutes, by another hill G4	
			H.A. Grimble Major. O.C. 63 M.G.C.	

MEMORANDUM.

From O.C. 63. M.G. Coy

To 37/C Bde

From

To

May 1st 1917.

War Diary of above unit for week of April - May, owing to active operations is delayed.

[Signature]
O.C. 63. M.G. Coy

ANSWER.

191

WAR DIARY
or
INTELLIGENCE SUMMARY

63rd Machine Gun Coy.

Army Form C. 2118.

Place	Date	Hour	Summary of Events and Information	Remarks and references to Appendices
GOUY-EN-TERNOIS.	1st April 1917		Coy at its Winter Quarters perfecting attacks to break forward.	
		7.15 AM	Coy left GOUY EN TERNOIS and marched with Brigade to MANIN arriving at billets abt 9 AM.	
	6th		Coy left and took the Brigade, practising the advance on a Brigade front.	
	7th	9 AM	Coy left MANIN marched to LATTRE ST QUENTIN – arriving 11 AM. Guns covering the Bde.	
	8th	8.30 AM	Coy left LATTRE ST QUENTIN marched with Brigade to DUISANS.	
	9th	5.30 AM	Gr marched direct to assembly trenches E of ARRAS. In ARRAS picking up feed etc to the Bde – arriving in assembly trenches abt midday.	
		1.15 PM	Reported Brigade HQ for order then rejoined Red & Blue objective Red Line Col. on Red ¾ No 8.19 (N? 3rd section) then to Blue Final III Bdjde Blue objective. Crumps position on ORANGE HILL. Immediately deposited No 2 section Blue position (H.35.a.2.1 × 5.9) preparatory to going forward for the 112th Brigade. This it also done – No 3rd section covered to a section abt H.21d.5.5 Coy under

WAR DIARY or INTELLIGENCE SUMMARY.

Army Form C. 2118.

63. M.G. Coy. 2.

Place	Date	Hour	Summary of Events and Information	Remarks and references to Appendices
			hostile M.G. fire from the German trenches running through H.34 a., there being no sign of our own Infantry in front of them - These two sections consequently withdrew to about H 27 a 2.3. until such time as it would be possible to take up their barrage positions on ORANGE HILL - Meanwhile on receipt of orders from the 63rd Bde that the Bde was to move forward from assembly trenches to BATTERY VALLEY, I issued orders to my 2 remaining sections (Nos 1 & 2) to advance thither - No 1 section to be in support & No 2 to be split up 2 guns with 8/S.L.I & 2 with 8/Lincolns. About 1.30 PM orders were issued for 8/SLI & 8/Lincolns to move forward through H 28., 8/S.L.I on the right & 8/Lincolns echeloned to their left rear - The 4 guns [No 2 section] split up as above moved with these Regts By 9 PM April 9th the positions of the sections were as follows - No 1 section in reserve in BATTERY VALLEY. Nos 3 & 4 sections about H 33 a 9.9. waiting for the line on ORANGE HILL to be established, so that they could move up to their barrage positions - No 2 section - 2 guns with 8/S.L.I & 2 with 8/Lincolns in H 28 b & d respectively -	

By 12 PM the Column was in contact with the enemy who the guns of 101 Bottle B.A.C. 175/8/this date had pushed further East with their infantry screen.

Mjhd 11 AM Orb. to 5' refuel that the had actd the valley running through H 30.b.12. - Surprisingly could show in No 3 sect. Artillery Brigade in their forward position on ORANGE HILL. - During the afternoon this guns were able to fire on enemy dried trafic in or about the high ground west of MONCHY LE PREUX. -

Mjhd 4.30 PM in the afternoon the bof Sgt Hopkin 1/c of the 2 guns attached to 81 Chochhshin Bttl. was considerable number of German defensive harroning fire N of the Oise at H.25.a. - Accordingly opened fire on this at a rate of one belt per gun attaining good cooperation. This destroy avoiding the former infantries infantry counter..

The 2 guns attached 8/5/15 remained field on outpost duty and taught a few men with the tank team sing sing btte. Firing shots at remainder, and second Lieuts. Vedmund, to brick decide ETA/D the fire

WAR DIARY or INTELLIGENCE SUMMARY

(4) 63. M.G. Co.

Army Form C. 2118.

should it be wanted in case of a counter attack —

By 12. mn 10th the guns were in the following positions
  No 1 Section in reserve in BATTERY VALLEY.
  No 2 " 2 guns approx H.30.C.8.8 & 2 guns approx H.36.a.3.8.
  No 3 & 4 Sections in their barrage positions on ORANGE HILL —

Shortly after midnight, orders were issued that the GREEN LINE was to be attacked at 5 AM on the 11th by the 15th Divn. & that the 37th Divn. was to pass through with the 63rd Bde in ~~reserve~~ Support — Accordingly Nos 7 & 8 groups opened fire at 5 AM as per barrage programme, but were unable to fire the prescribed number of rounds owing to the rapidity of the advance & the difficulty of observation on our own troops —

Meanwhile No 1 section advanced to H.28.c.3.7. where it was ordered to halt —
At about 10 AM this section again moved forward, picking up No 3 section on its way, both sections taking up a position about H.35.b.3.5. &
No 4 section on ORANGE HILL coming into reserve as per programme —
About 3 PM I received orders that the river & its N bank in H.25 a & b.

Place	Date	Hour	Summary of Events and Information	Remarks and references to Appendices
			Until the attack started – I at once dispatched No 3 ladder to guard the position H. 30. c. 7. 3. — meanwhile No 4 ladder in reserve at H.35 a 9.1. The guns outside Bapaume to cover the high ground in N 6a. One of Divisional Cavalry rejoined there. The 4 guns A.T.? sub. Bing respectively in pairs about H. 36c S.S.9– H.36 f 8.9. — No 1 Ladr. Being prepared to advance both 8/5.1 & 1st day & Lar a firm. H 36 d 5.4.	
		6 a.m. 1st	Received orders from Bde. aren. by GS H FEUCHY CHAPEL RED.1 — this have been completed by midday –	
ARRAS –		4 pm	At 4 pm H. Qrs. moved from her Chalets in ARRAS – Throughout the afternoon the nature have reminded quite uni... air raids. Hoursie Rd to our Advanced Schools full of men, very heavy casualties. Nile rolls funding. –	
			I gave the the there forward instructions under cover of night & this had dang of [?]	
			II Saloon horsed in the Tram Depot stable in case expected furthen to also p.t.	
		2 a 8 hrs. –		

WAR DIARY or INTELLIGENCE SUMMARY. 63 Machine Gun Coy

Army Form C. 2118.

Place	Date	Hour	Summary of Events and Information	Remarks and references to Appendices

			III M.G. barrage fire would be easier to control & generally more satisfactory if Bde M.Gs covered their own front - because.
			     a. The dispositions of one's own Brigade, if they can not actually be seen can be easily, or comparatively easily found out - whereas the dispositions of other Brigades can rarely be seen & are infinitely harder to ascertain -
			     b. Brigades naturally prefer their own guns to be firing over them & the M. gunners themselves naturally find it easier to keep in touch with their own Brigades -
			 IV Large carrying parties absolutely essential - Gun teams to be made up to at least 10 men per gun (in toto) -
			 V Very great difficulty in spotting hostile M guns & engaging them -
			 VI Difficulty of rationing the various sections which are of necessity scattered all over the Bde front, & the suggestion that in cases where M. guns are attached to Regts that those Regts ration the M. gunners -
			 VII The desirability of a Field Kitchen
			 VIII The difficulty of keeping belts dry in the present belt box (as issued) during bad weather. -	

WAR DIARY
INTELLIGENCE SUMMARY

63. Machine Gun Coy

Place	Date	Hour	Summary of Events and Information	Remarks and references to Appendices
ARRAS	13th	2.30 pm	Coy marched to Lattrecies in DUISANS -	
DUISANS	14th	11.30 am	Coy arrived with the Brigade Headquarters in AGNES DUISANS	
AGNES DUISANS	15th	9/15	Coy marched with the Brigade to BEAUFORT & fields - weather cold & depressing.	
			G.O.C. 37th Div inspected the Brigade on the 16 Funds -	
	17th		Coy marched with the Brigade in MARIAN was billeted at BEAUCOURT - warning was "stand by"	
			When it moved to MONTENESCOURT, was there for one night 21st August	
MONTENESCOURT	14th		Coy marched to the river N of the SCARPE west of ARRAS to belong our four M.G.R Coy.	
			It left o/c the Coy (Major Green) has relief Brigade M.G. Officer	
	20th		Coy went into the line. The 16 M.G. Coy remaining in the line also	
	21st 1919		Considerable hostile shelling	
	23rd		Maxm. 4.15 am 8 guns at the Coy [?] in bombarded enemy line in preparation	
			Fairly heavy enemy front line shell of artillery barrage. In other Barrage & heavy enemy barrage like our troops to advanced. In the Bois d'Achille from the factory	
			West 2 northern approach & HSL TI 18/ [?] at 2 am on this line the forward battalions of the 63rd Brigade pin the two Coys.	
			Line with 2 miles ended to here through GREENLAND HILL - passed left & the [?]	

WAR DIARY
or
INTELLIGENCE SUMMARY.
(Erase heading not required.)

Army Form C. 2118.

(8)

63.M.9.Co2

Place	Date	Hour	Summary of Events and Information	Remarks and references to Appendices
	23rd	10.AM	These 2 sections ordered to move in irregular formation – (teams in Echelon), half an hour interval between sections to a line 200" W of X Rd in I.7.a. – route followed HERON Tr over the open toward CHEMICAL WORKS. – When clear of HYDERABAD Redt to make for position allotted turning N.E. – 2 guns being detailed for defence of right flank. The manner in which section officers carried out these orders & worked their teams through German barrage in perfect regularity reflects the greatest credit on section & team commanders for their coolness & control.	
		12.NN/PM	Situation as above for the forward sections – No 4 section had lost its officer, 2 guns & half its personnel & was in reserve 500x E. of HYDERABAD Redt – No 3 section was out of touch with 8/Lincolns – consequently these 2 sections formed the forward reserve – 1 & 2 sections being forward with the Infy. Meanwhile an ominous absence of movement on the W. slopes of GREENLAND HILL & enemy activity behind it – OC Coy therefore in company with OC York & Lancaster Bn made a reconnaissance of the Right flank from FAMPOUX to X Rd I.7.a. – A few Middlesex & York men at dressing station about HYDERABAD Redt non cognisant of the situation of their various Regts. 6/Seaforths advancing up CAM Tr – their officers did not know where the Infy advanced line was (Bn on our Right)	

WAR DIARY
or
INTELLIGENCE SUMMARY.

(Erase heading not required.)

Army Form C. 2118.

(9.)

63. M.G. Coÿ

Instructions regarding War Diaries and Intelligence Summaries are contained in F. S. Regs., Part II. and the Staff Manual respectively. Title pages will be prepared in manuscript.

Place	Date	Hour	Summary of Events and Information	Remarks and references to Appendices
			CADIX T⁰ lightly held by some of our Inf⁷ with some German prisoners –	
		1.30th	8 Guns (1 & 2 sections & what was left of N⁰ 3 section = 8 guns in all) ⁴ in position on a line parallel to R⁰ from about H.12.b.9.9 to I.7.c.5.8 ⁴ on R⁰ flanged their line in touch with 8/S.L.1. these guns commanded the whole of the W. slope of GREENLAND HILL – as Infantry had had heavy losses ʳ 3 Co's knocked out, they were in no definite positions at all but were more or less scattered about in shell holes – very heavy hostile shelling – though generally speaking they were on the 2ⁿᵈ objective, the blue line –	
		1.35th	German Counter attack impending – Inf⁷ did not seem the in touch with each other seemed too few to withstand an attack.	
			1ˢᵗ attempted Counter attack –	
			3 waves of Germans advancing over Greenland hill in lines about 800ˣ in length – all 8 guns opened fire on these lines traversing inwards, despite heavy German M.gun covering fire – attack Completely broken – & a great number of Casualties inflicted, in fact the attack completely wiped out – our artillery was not firing at the time as there seemed to be some doubt amongst their O.P's whether or no it might be our own men retiring.	
			2ⁿᵈ attempted Counter attack	

T2134. Wt. W708 –776. 500030. 4/15. Sir J. C. & S.

WAR DIARY or INTELLIGENCE SUMMARY

(10.) 63. M.G. Coy (10.)

Army Form C. 2118.

Place	Date	Hour	Summary of Events and Information	Remarks and references to Appendices
			In closer formation of greater depth, this only provided a still better target & was dealt with in if possible a more satisfactory manner than the 1st attempt - hundreds of casualties being inflicted - meanwhile 2 of our guns knocked out & several casualties from both German artillery fire which was very heavy & M. Gun fire -	
	9th	dark	Germans dribbling down Greenland Hill in 1's & 2's - many killed by our M.G. fire. Infantry did not use their rifles nearly enough -	
		6.30 P.m	112th Inf Bde attacked for final objective Brown Line, they had to advance over 2000' of open in full view & never really passed through 63rd Bde on account of the very heavy & accurate barrage Germans put up - During this afternoon 8 guns mentioned above fired over 12,000 rounds - & did enormous damage - but for these guns I am convinced the 2 counter attacks would have been successful - this was realised by the Infantry themselves who could not do enough to add to the comfort of our men provided they shared with them !-	
		8 P.m	Guns re-arranged after reconnaissance by Lt Webb & myself - 2 guns being posted on either flank of 63rd Inf Bde about I.7.c.7.8 & I.7.a.4.6 respectively - 2 guns in support H.12.d.8.3. - (1 & 3 sections) - 2 guns (No 4 section) & 8 men H.12.c.7.8.	

Place	Date	Hour	Summary of Events and Information	Remarks and references to Appendices
	24th		Men during hours of daylight in cists & advanced trench trench works attached. Our L.G.'s prevented should attem- [?] /12 June the two 1st line two tie & attem- pts placed our efforts these rounds to explode. Me Turks adding Painful not having caught their own fund two has repeatedly not shelling our zim heavily.	
	4 P.M.		A number of figures seen in GREENLAND HILL the food of by us. Guns, Rumple. We are within actable trench about. - It seem inclined -	
	11.30 P.M.		G.O.C. to let the Brigade actions the Heads - A HERON T8 to open fire - 24 which two out of action from shell fire / Broad comp. for t Shales -	
			Commanced a HERON T8 Hn 27th	
	27th		Heavy rain fr 4.15 a. 285 Effective output from the - All ranks much 4 killed shelters - Battalion for outre fr ever T8 - 2 Koln in ford 2 H. support - 9 time others over the whole ford (8 time 11 H & G's 8 112. 16. 19) hrs G's offers Inspector frame / 8/11.5 + L medic. workshops - It 11 pm & 2nd open attacks in G's supports - Few shells 8/111 + Shrato in frontier. 2 Pm. 28/4/17 - At 4.25 Pm two the 14/4 + 18/4 from the class of Cpls Punch. Hn Piven. Larsan johns. (illegible) his on taking for land - in safely attacked Friebel trench returned in d

WAR DIARY
or
INTELLIGENCE SUMMARY. (12.)
(Erase heading not required.)

Army Form C. 2118.

63. M.G. Coy

Place	Date	Hour	Summary of Events and Information	Remarks and references to Appendices
			for about 100ˣ when the attack was hung up by the failure of the Divⁿ on our right to take the Chemical Works, & consequent enfilade M.G. fire.	
			The 4 guns attached Infy therefore took cover 50ˣ behind the leading Infy, in shell holes but as the field of fire was not so good from there as from CUTHBERT Tʳ they withdrew to that trench, enabling them a better field of fire, better observation etc. These guns remained here under heavy shell fire & sniping, & incurred many casualties. Position of our Infy on the right not clear.	
			These guns however got into action on small german targets during the day & did good work in keeping down enemy sniping. Our Infantry had suffered heavily, there was no definite line held, simply isolated shell holes. Situation on the right very precarious & obscure. One might almost put it at general confusion amongst both ourselves & the enemy.	
			The 4 Vickers & 4 Lewis guns in Coy Support were in position in CHRI Tʳ from I.12.c.9.1 to I.18.c.7.8 at 3.30 AM where they remained all day, getting into action on to small german counter attacks between 12.30 & 1.30 PM & 8 & 9 PM, 4000 rounds being fired by these guns & no counter attacks therefore maturing.	

The Fd Amb Bury attended put Befri dues -

Order Issued 98E under instructions for Brigade. To It Shers Guns attac 63M.G.Co
Bn Hdrs are to 91A Haff -

Order night of 28E May See attacks by 28E Hy Br Machine Gun brens
unworking in the the night of 28E Btn. May has deeply with down -

The Commander congratulates the Co "A" the magnificent work of this Machine Gun
Coanadia scored the am. Army - 2E1 during all 3 attacks sustained in the days
fighting attacks in). 6 officers + 77 O.R. -

H.A. Colwell Major.
OC 63rd Machine Gun Co.

WAR DIARY or INTELLIGENCE SUMMARY (Erase heading not required.)

Army Form C. 2118.

63. M.G. Coy

Vol 15

Place	Date	Hour	Summary of Events and Information	Remarks and references to Appendices
MANIN	May 1st		Coy remained in MANIN from May 1st to 18th. Reequippment carried out & some 50 reinforcements received also 4 officer reinforcements - unfortunately none of these men have had previous war experience. A considerable amount of training range practice carried out. The training consisting chiefly of semi open & open fighting - Infy Drill & gun Drill carried out.	
SIMENCOURT	18th	10.35am	Coy moved to SIMENCOURT - route - NOYELLE VION - LATTRE St QUENTIN WANQUENTIN arriving in billet 2pm. Brigade march.	
DAINVILLE	19th	1.50pm	Coy marched to DAINVILLE via DOULENES Rd arriving 3pm. (brigade march). Coy remained here 20th	
ARRAS.	21st	12 noon	Coy moved to ARRAS & billeted there -	
	22nd		4 officers sent up to reconnoitre line to be taken over - (line running from MONCHY LE PREUX to CASOLE River - very wet day -	
"	23rd		Coy. remained in billets. Training carried on. New men were taken round the old front line system, & trench warfare & transition to open warfare were explained to them by experienced Officers & N.C.O.'s.	
"	24th			
"	25th			

WAR DIARY or INTELLIGENCE SUMMARY.

(Erase heading not required.)

Army Form C. 2118.

63rd M.G. Coy.

Place	Date	Hour	Summary of Events and Information	Remarks and references to Appendices
ARRAS	26		Train carried on i.e. Division accounts etc.	
"	27th		Church service in Morning. Afternoon clean up. Company move to Tilloy. Ready to take over from 111th Coy.	
Tilloy	29		Coy resting in Barracks & coming out Vespers. Coy Specialists under Barrage at Home. F.O.O. parties out as per Instructions from G.O. Coy moves to ARKHS at 9 o'clock. Orders for move to MANIN received. Section return from line.	
ARRAS	31			

8 Wallace Lt
for O.C. 63 M.G. Coy.

SECRET

16

M/Sgt Many
63rd M.G. Con
June 1917

"A" Form.

MESSAGES AND SIGNALS.

Army Form C.2121
(in pads of 100).

No. of Message

Prefix	Code	Words	Charge		This message is on a/c of:
Office of Origin					........................Service,
Service Instructions		Sent			
		At	m.		
		To			....
		By			(Signature of "Franking Officer.")

Recd. at	m.
Date	
From	
By	

TO { 37th Division Q

Sender's Number.	Day of Month.	In reply to Number.	AAA

aw 21 | 30th |

Herewith War Diary for month of June for
63rd M.G. Coy.

To O'Rielly, A. for
OC. 63rd M.G. Coy

From
Place
Time

*This line should be erased if not required.

WAR DIARY or INTELLIGENCE SUMMARY.

Army Form C. 2118.

63. M.G. Coy

Place	Date	Hour	Summary of Events and Information	Remarks and references to Appendices
ARRAS	June 1st		Coy embussed from ARRAS & moved to MANIN.	
MANIN	2nd		All Coy's kit & equipment thoroughly overhauled.	
	3rd		New Draft exercised on the range.	
	4th		Company training.	
	5th		Coy marched to BEAUFORT for embussing to SIRACOURT.	
	6th		Coy marched to ANVIN.	
	7th		" " RADINGHEM.	
	8th		Coy training	
	9th		Coy marched to HEZECQUES, where it billeted —	

WAR DIARY or INTELLIGENCE SUMMARY

63 M.G. Coy.

Place	Date	Hour	Summary of Events and Information	Remarks and references to Appendices
HEZECQUES	June 19th		Company remained in HEZECQUES from June 19th to 22nd. Class order drill, range practice, musketry drill were carried out. Extra lecturing & training are practised. On 19th, the honours are notified by the G.O.C. - Secret sitting. On 21st a distribution towards the place in FRUGES. The recipients are 2/Lt W.R. WEBB (M.C.), 2/Lt N.F. HAWES (M.C.), Sergt HUGHES (D.C.M.), Sergt YATES (M.M.), Sergt CROSS (M.M.). The last named N.C.O. was previously awarded the D.C.M.	
RELY	22nd		The Company moved to RELY via BEAUMETZ-LEZ-AIRE, FEBVIN, arriving in billets at 2.30. pm	to shelters
STEENBECQUE	23rd		The Company moved to STEEN BECQUE via AIRE, arriving in billets at 9am. There were no shoppings. Livestock were unattended as reported.	(80 miles)
ST.SILVESTRE CAPPEL	24th		The Company moved to ST.SILVESTRE CAPPEL, via HAZEBROUCK, arriving in billets at 9am. There are no shoppings.	
KLONDYKE FARM	25th	9.5ᵗ	The Coy marched to KLONDYKE FARM (N.19.c.05.) Sheet 28 S.W. There were no shoppings, although the march was a severe test.	
		9.15ᵗ	From 26th to 28th, Equipment, Gun kit, and personal kit inspected. Gas drill carried out each day. On the 26th the O.C. Coy and Adjutant reconnoitred the line	
		2.7ᵗ	The Officer i/c of transport reconnoitred positions for teams	
		28ᵗ	The Coy took over the line on the WYTSCHAETE Ridge. Key teams were during relief Troop H.Q. until English 11 am —	
		29ᵗ	Every action was likely in fact was — The weather was very active, on the 29th firing considerable & of cases of the link to afford until 1 Gas shelter is rather safest place — About four minutes much after midnight, making much difficulty. So far, Lewis key fork charges fired —

WAR DIARY or INTELLIGENCE SUMMARY

Army Form C. 2118.

63. M.G. Coy

Place	Date	Hour	Summary of Events and Information	Remarks and references to Appendices
In the Line	30th	3.30 AM	Gun positions visited by O.C. & 2/I/C - heavy rain - hostile artillery very much less active than on the 29th - usual method of Enemy shelling is unsystematic, shells being flung about indiscriminately, with the exception of sudden & systematic bursts of fire on our battery positions.	

W.G.A. Coldwell Major.
O.C. 63 Machine Gun Coy

War Diary
65 Machine Gun Co
JULY 1917

WAR DIARY or INTELLIGENCE SUMMARY.

(Erase heading not required.)

Army Form C. 2118.

63 M.G. Coy

Place	Date	Hour	Summary of Events and Information	Remarks and references to Appendices
	July 1st		Company in the line O.16.A.7.9. to O.22.B.2.3. harassing fire on tracks and roads behind enemy front line.	
	2		Company in the line, harassing fire as on the 1st.	
	3		Company relieved by the 59th M.G.Coy at 11.50pm. Transport moved from N.9.b. central (Sheet 28 – 10000) to Donegal Farm. N.31.D.	
Donegal Farm	4th		Cleaning of guns, gun kit, equipment etc.	
" "	5th		General cleaning up of mens clothing, hair-cutting & boots repaired. Respirators examined & drill carried out. No 4 Section attached to 111th Coy in the line.	
" "	6th		Training - specialists classes for range-takers, scouts, signallers & physical training; gun drill, indirect fire drill.	
" "	7th		Section which had been attached to 111th M.G.Coy rejoined Company.	

WAR DIARY
or
INTELLIGENCE SUMMARY

63 M.G.Coy

Army Form C. 2118.

Place	Date	Hour	Summary of Events and Information	Remarks and references to Appendices
Kemmel	July 1st		Training continued, inspection of kits & equipment. M.G. position for defence of MESSINES – WYTCHAETE Ridge reconnoitred.	
"	" 8th		Church Parade.	
"	" 15th		Training continued. Parades daily. Lecture on indents for Limbers packed, orders re Relics ill ** M.G. Coy in the line.	
"	" 16th		022 b 3.3 to 035 A 2.99s. Relief complete 12.30.a.m. 16 guns in position forming two lines of defence for Brigade. (a) Barrage line from 12 guns along approaches from front held by enemy. (b) Close fire from all 16 guns of enemy fast through front line system. A third line of defence formed by 19th M.G. Coy occupying positions on the Ridge.	

WAR DIARY
or
INTELLIGENCE SUMMARY.
(Erase heading not required.)

Army Form C. 2118.

63 M.G. Coy

Place	Date	Hour	Summary of Events and Information	Remarks and references to Appendices
	July 12		In the line, co-operation with the artillery, harassing fire employed at night against farms, posts, tracks & routes used by the enemy. Work on emplacements, shelters for the gun teams carried out.	
	13th		In the line, work carried out as above.	
	14th		Guns directed on target engaged by artillery during the day. No movement observed. Harassing fire at night on the usual targets behind enemy's line of posts.	
	15th		One section of 112th M.G.C. replaced left section of this Coy. Left section moved over to right of Brigade front to positions near Angac Farm. Emplacements & shelters constructed. Programme for remaining three sections same as on 14th.	

WAR DIARY
or
INTELLIGENCE SUMMARY.

(Erase heading not required.)

Army Form C. 2118.

Place	Date	Hour	Summary of Events and Information	Remarks and references to Appendices
In line	July 16		Positions for indian Jews constructed near ANZAC FARM. Measuring jig on forms. Finish a pair shell by	
"	17			
"	18th		Orders issued (O.O.111) for attack of a daylight raid to measure in conjunction with B Battery tomorrow. Rifle pere on 2nd by one minimum of the Barrage against RIFLE FARM. All the guns of the Company to co-operate by putting up barrage. Order for guns completed and sent to Section.	
"	19th		Raid cancelled, O.O.116 for relief of 63rd Brigade by 112th Brigade. Measuring jig carried out on night opposite the more corps. Eight positions and slits for Jules Iran division complete in the neighbourhood of ANZAC FARM.	

WAR DIARY or **INTELLIGENCE SUMMARY.**

Army Form C. 2118.

63 MGCoy

Place	Date	Hour	Summary of Events and Information	Remarks and references to Appendices
In Line	July 20th		Dump of S.A.A. completed near gun positions. Work on improvement of positions continued and the usual programme of fire carried out.	
Donegal Farm	21st		Company relieved in the line by 112th Coy. Relief complete 12.30 a.m. Sections marched to Donegal Farm.	
"	" 22nd		Church Parades, cleaning of guns equipment etc.	
"	" 23rd		Training – Physical training, squad drill and lectures on Indirect Fire. Extensions to Box Respirators fitted.	
"	" 24th		Training Physical Training, Squad Drill. Lectures on use of traversing dial and explanations of "Late Stop" and use of Clinometer. Respirator Drill	

WAR DIARY
or
INTELLIGENCE SUMMARY.
(Erase heading not required.)

Army Form C. 2118.

Place	Date	Hour	Summary of Events and Information	Remarks and references to Appendices
	September 24		Training - Platoon training. Squad drill, cleaning of equipment. Orders received making outdoor work impossible. Lecture in picture palace. No.3 Section went into the line attached to B Company for operations.	
	" 26		Preparations made for going into the line by the Company.	
	" 27		Standing by orders to shift camp. The order was altered & camp shifted into the next field.	
	" 28		Training - Platoon training. Lecture W. Wasilowiecki. Kit inspection.	
	" 29		Church Parade. Remainder of day Company moved into preparations for going into the line for operations.	

A5834 Wt.W.4973/M687 750,000 8/16 D.D.&L.Ltd. Forms/C.2118/13.

WAR DIARY
              or
     INTELLIGENCE SUMMARY.   63 M.G Coy
        (Erase heading not required.)

Army Form C. 2118.

Place	Date	Hour	Summary of Events and Information	Remarks and references to Appendices
Inline	30th		Company in line for operations, these details will will be reported in next months diary.	

W.G.A. Coldwell Major
Commanding No. 63 M.G. Coy.
Machine Gun Corps.

War Diary
63rd M.G. Coy
Aug 1917

81

WAR DIARY
or
INTELLIGENCE SUMMARY.
(Erase heading not required.)

Army Form C. 2118.

63rd M.G. Coy   Map References
WYTSCHAETE 1/10000
Ed. 6a.

Place	Date	Hour	Summary of Events and Information	Remarks and references to Appendices
In the line	July 30		Sector E. of WYTSCHAETE. N° 2 and a half section of N° 1 took up positions for barrage fire in conjunction with 111th, 112th and 247th M.G. Coys for active operations. N° 3 Section attached to the infantry, N° 4 in support at GUN FARM*¹ and a half section of N° 1 in reserve*² and on A.A. work.	at O.28.A. 20.15. *¹ O.27.A.85.80. *² O.20.B.30.20.
" " "	31		Barrage fire carried out and from reports with good results, harassing fire carried out throughout the day.	
" " "	Aug 1		Harassing fire continued. N° 3 Section withdrawn from infantry and sent down to BULLY BEEF FARM*³ to re-equip etc. men in a very bad state owing to bad weather conditions.	*³ N.29.C.15.90. *⁴ position at O.27.B.90.30
" " "	2		Barrage line taken over by N° 4 Section from positions near "GUN FARM"*⁴ on account of the other positions falling in owing to the bad weather and consistent hostile shelling. N° 2 & half section of N° 1 withdrawn to reserve positions.	

Robert E. Read
Major

WAR DIARY
or
INTELLIGENCE SUMMARY

Army Form C. 2118.

629 July 1917

Place	Date	Hour	Summary of Events and Information	Remarks and references to Appendices
In line	Aug 3		Harassing fire carried out. Company withdrew at night to BULLY BEEF FARM. (Fm.s D'HOINE) Whilst with BSOJYS Canadian Army Corps for instructional work in Engineers duties, Company received orders from 3rd Australian Field Coys and rejoined and Company marched to LOCRE HOF FARM. DRANOUTRE, where the men were rebilletted.	x N⁰.24c.15.90
	4			x N⁰.29 D.3.1. Shoots 25.S.W/1000
" "	7		Church parade. Fine day. 16 N.C.Os and Warrants Officers for overhaul. N⁰.3¼ Section went into the line East of WYTSCHAETE with line section of N⁰.247 For. UC. 63 Pm in command, wire clothing exchanged.	x N⁰.3¼ Section at O.21.C.90.00
" "	8		Fire section in the line. Harassing carried out by the Howitzers. Fire section P.I Bus 2.Ld at 2h in the morning. Preparations made in the afternoon to go into the line with fire section of 112 M.Gs. fire section at night N.E of WYTSCHAETE¼ OC 112 Coy in command.	x N⁰.2 Section at O.15.D.30.60. N⁰.1 Section at O.I.C.70.60.
			N⁰.3¼ Section refilled by 12¼ Australian M.G Coy and went into Reserve Billets at La Petite Ferme.x⁵ N⁰.1.92 Section in the line. N⁰.3¼ section consolidating Iron K.B.D. fire section in line, harassing fire carried out on an reserve target fire section in Reserve training and finding working parties.	x⁵ N⁰.213.30.84 Shoot 25 S.W/1000
	9¼		La Petite Ferme	

SLD 19¼/Q
HEADQUARTERS
dd13¼/Q

WAR DIARY or INTELLIGENCE SUMMARY

Army Form C. 2118.

63 Coy M.G.C

Place	Date	Hour	Summary of Events and Information	Remarks and references to Appendices
La Polka Farm	Aug 11		Two sections in line harassing fire as before. Two sections in reserve training and finding working parties.	
" " "	12		Same as the 11th	
" " "	13		On the night of 13th the two sections in line were relieved by 112" M.G. Coy and withdrew to La Polka Farm.	
" " "	14		Cleaning up and overhauling gun kit.	
" " "	15		Training. At night N°s 3 & 4 sections went into line with two sections of 247 P.T. N°3 at ROSEWOOD O.16.a.70.70. N°4 at DENYSWOOD O.9.D.72.28.	
" " "	16		Two sections in the line, remaining two training and finding working parties	
" " "	17		As for 16th.	
" " "	18		As for 17th.	
" " "	19		As for 18th.	
" " "	20		As for 19th.	
" " "	21		As for 20th.	

Edw. McDeed
Major

WAR DIARY or INTELLIGENCE SUMMARY

Army Form C. 2118.

Place	Date	Hour	Summary of Events and Information	Remarks and references to Appendices
La Cateau	Aug 22		At night two sections in firing line relieved by 113th MG Coy 2 sections to Reserve Billets	
"	" 23		Cleaning up and overhauling gun kits	
"	" 24		Training. D.1 Gun died out	
"	" 25		Training	
"	" 26		Company relieved by 111th MG Coy and moved back to M.81.B.5.3. Billets.	Gun Positions Military 286.27.1.17 0.15.15
M.81.B.5.3	" 27		Training	
"	" 28		Company ordered to go into the line, HOLLEBEKE Sector, action moved in the evening by bus and relieved 111th MG Coy	
In the line	" 29		Company in the line	No 2. 0.11.a.10.05 0.15.75.15
"	" 30		Harassing fire carried out on "	B.11.20.20 0.11.20.20
"	" 31		Practice barrage in co-operation with 1st Artillery.	No 3, Barenghaus 0.11.a.6.60
"	" "		Harassing fire carried out.	M.2.H.C.A. 0.15.65
			Casualties for the month 21 wounded, 16 R.vers died of wounds 1 Officer wounded 1 Officer sick – to hospital. Maj F Elliott M.C.	

63 Coy MGC

Vol 19

WAR DIARY
or
INTELLIGENCE SUMMARY

Army Form C. 2118.

63rd Coy, M.G.C.

Place	Date	Hour	Summary of Events and Information	Remarks and references to Appendices
HOLLEBEKE SECTOR	1916 Sept 1		Work on improvement of shelter and improvements. Barrage fire 2 hours, part carried out by the Barrage on our right.	Details of firing on attached during Report. APPENDIX A.
"	2		Further improvement work during the day, and by such hours as were not under observation; Harassing fire carried out at night, in co-operation with the Artillery. The section on A.A. were relieved under orders from Brigade by gun teams of the 9 (North) Staffordshire Regt, the action thus relieved keep up barrages at O.11.A.30.90. O.11.A.29.95. O.30.c.05. and O.30.c.30.10. in order to strengthen the fire defence.	
"	3		Harassing fire carried out at night.	
"	4		Work on improvements carried out; harassing fire carried out at night.	
"	4½		Work on improvements carried out; harassing fire carried out at night.	
"	5		Gun at O.E.c.20.10.10 knocked out by shrapnel (Burst every immediate) This gun was replaced by our team at O.11.A.90.30. Usual work on improvement and harassing fire at night.	
"	6		Work on improvement carried out. Orders received for the Company to be relieved by the 11th M.G. Coy on 7th inst. Relief complete[?]	

WAR DIARY
or
INTELLIGENCE SUMMARY.

63rd Coy, M.G. Corps.

Army Form C. 2118.

Place	Date	Hour	Summary of Events and Information	Remarks and references to Appendices
In the line	Sept 6th cont		At 11.0 p.m., Company moved to camp previously occupied by 111th M.G. Coy. Casualties during this period in the line - Nil.	
N.10.C.	7		Company moved to camp in N.10.C., tents erected & general work on forming camp.	
N.10.C.	8		Overhauling Gun Kit and cleaning up generally.	
N.10.C.	9		Squad Drill & Church parades. Warning order received to move.	
M.13.B.9.9	11th		Company marched from camp at N.10.C. to camp at M.13.B.9.9 BOESCHEPPE training area.	
M.13.B.9.9	11th		Training. P.T. Company drill, Gun drill, Squad drill etc. Afternoon devoted to recreation.	
M.13.B.9.9	12		Training. P.T. Company drill. Mechanism, Indication and recognition of targets etc. Afternoon, Gun & personal kit inspection	
M.13.B.9.9	13		Training. P.T. Company drill Mechanism S.A. etc Afternoon recreation.	

Major

WAR DIARY
or
INTELLIGENCE SUMMARY

Army Form C. 2118.

63rd Coy. M.G. C/c.

Place	Date	Hour	Summary of Events and Information	Remarks and references to Appendices
M.10.b.9.9.	14		Company drill and Musketry at Afternoon - recreation.	
M.10.b.9.9.	15		P.T. Company drill. Lecture signal and to Afternoon recreation	
M.10.b.9.9.	16		Church Parade.	
M.10.b.9.9.	17		Lecture on the enemy. Remarks of Army Company drill, Musketry and drill concerning of mounting of gun on ancrew ground etc.	
M.13.b.8.9.	18th		Warning order received for Company to be prepared to move at 2 hours notice. Training carried out in my Vickers Shoot. At 10 p.m. 63rd A.A. Bn. O.O. No 162 received. Company ordered to move on the 19th inst. to the FAIRY HOUSE area (nr BRULOOZE, Shed 28 S.W.). Company to march separately all ranks to be held in readiness to move off from No 102 billets within two hours of receipt of necessary orders.	
Shed 28 S.W.	19th		Pre arranged billeting arrangements completed by 2 p.m. Company left camp at M.13.b.8.9. at 4.30 p.m. passed starting point (M.23.a.25.60) at 4.15 p.m. Company arrived in new camp at HEMMEL SHELTERS at 10 p.m. men at 10.30 p.m. Motor lorry used for carriage of blankets & others.	
N.16.d.	"		Hours (roughly) a sand bag drawn from YORK HOUSE N.16.d.93. for use in the event of the Coy needing into action. Coy of supplies forwarded to the HQ behind in accordance with S.S. 135 forwarded to 13th H.Q.	

[signature] Maj.

WAR DIARY
or
INTELLIGENCE SUMMARY.
(Erase heading not required.)

Army Form C. 2118.

63rd Coy, M.G. Corps.

Instructions regarding War Diaries and Intelligence Summaries are contained in F.S. Regs., Part II. and the Staff Manual respectively. Title pages will be prepared in manuscript.

Place	Date	Hour	Summary of Events and Information	Remarks and references to Appendices
N.19 d central	20th		Training carried out in vicinity of camp — Range taking, making of range cards, infantry and gun drill.	
N.19 d "	21st	4.30pm	Warning order received at 11 a.m. for Company to be prepared to move at one hours notice. Training suspended. 63rd Inf Bde. O.O. No. 163 received. Bde. to march back to Mt KOKEREELE area, & units to occupy same billets as before. Company passed starting point — HYDE PARK CORNER, M.14.c. at 6.5 p.m. and arrived in camp M.13.b.8.9 at 7 p.m.	
M.13 b 8.9.	22nd	10.30am	Company paraded, full marching order, for inspection by the G.O.C. Bde. At 11 a.m. inspection was cancelled and an order received to be ready to move at two hours notice. An officer and party were sent forward to reconnoitre the forward area near the BRASSERIE in N.6.a., prior to taking over from the 114th Bde. Order to move cancelled at 3.30 p.m., & units instructed to continue training.	
"	23rd		Church parades followed by inspection by O.C. Coy. At 2.30pm an inspection of the company was held by the G.O.C. Bde. Dress — full marching order.	
"	24th		Training continued. Firing on the range by one section, rough ground drill with limbers & pack transport by remainder at R.12.C.8.3. Physical training, gun drill & lecture on fire direction. A period of six hours occupied by this training.	
"	25th		Programme of training as on the previous day. Lecture given to sections on methods of fire.	
"	26th		Training continued as on the previous day. A different section firing each day on the range.	
"	27th		Training restricted to neighbourhood of the camp. Orders received from Bde. to be ready to move at one hour's notice. Remainder of Bde. moved forward at night to take over the line east of SHREWSBURY Forest from the 118th Bde. Reconnaissance carried out by each unit during the morning, troops transported in buses to BRICKSTACKS in I.33.c. (Sheet 28 S.W. BELGIUM)	
"	28th		Company carried in buses to camp at N.3.d.15.45, leaving M.13.b.8.9 at 4 a.m. Transport moved independently. At 1.30 pm the C.O. with 3 officers left camp to take over positions occupied by the 118th M.G. Coy. They proceeded to Coy HQrs. at Mount Sorrel I.30.a.88.15. The 11 guns and teams were put into two barrage positions; 6 guns at J.25.a.62.30 and 5 at J.25.b.34.44. This was carried out with no casualties, the teams taking in their own S.A.A. The accommodation was reported as poor at both positions chiefly consisting of shelters which are scarcely splinter proof.	

John McDiarmid Lieut

WAR DIARY or INTELLIGENCE SUMMARY

Army Form C. 2118.

Place	Date	Hour	Summary of Events and Information	Remarks and references to Appendices
M15 $\frac{1}{2}$-89	Sept 28 enroute	4.5 pm	An officer with 5 guns and Coy HQ taken over positions held by No 118 Coy at J26a 3245, J26a 5570, J26a 7288 and J26b 7350 (29 guns) These are now carried out nightly No cannelli at Conm batteries in this area S.A.A. being reported carried on rifle pin. Weather fine.	Details of Rifles on Anti-Aircraft Gun
I30 0 8815	Sept 29		Nothing of great importance occurred. Rifles were manned regularly by Section Officers. Firing was carried out on SOS lines and attention to pin attitude. The portions of the 3-guns post team at J26b7350 was even accurately located on J 26b 1060. Shots were carried out on all the gun positions and were infinite as far as possible. Weather was good, misty in early morning, bright sunshine during the day. Casualties: 1 man wounded.	Report attached Appendix B
"	Sept 30		Enemy artillery was very active during the day. Firing was carried out as required on attitude, bracelets, S.O.S lines with normal sensitivity under Controller. 1 Officer (2/Lt Ramsey) 3 men wounded. Ammunition was dispersed by transport from at J 25/A 62-30 to our rear lines near the firing. The fine forward guns were not to withdrawn at dusk, were to still to assist the Infantry in case of an enemy attack. On Sept 30 at 11pm orders to leave advance positions, enemy counter offensive on the enemy were received after the night is attention.	

Rutland Russell
Major

WAR DIARY
or
INTELLIGENCE SUMMARY.
(Erase heading not required.)

Army Form C. 2118.

Place	Date	Hour	Summary of Events and Information	Remarks and references to Appendices
J.30.A.85.15	Sept 30.		On the night of the 28/29th, of September 1917 the 37th Division Machine Guns established a defensive S.O.S. barrage line from J.27.c.45-25 to J.22.a.45-00. 16 guns of our Divisional Company the 244 Coy took from J.27.c.45-25 to J.27.b.55-45. 8 guns of our Company the 63 Coy took from J.27.b.45-54 to J.22.c.02-40 and 8 guns of the 111th Coy on our left Bde Sector took from J.21.d.9-2 to J.22.a.45-00. The guns of the 244 Coy are placed in the 111 Infy Bde area although they cover our right front.	

Major

WAR DIARY
or
INTELLIGENCE SUMMARY.
(Erase heading not required.)

Army Form C. 2118.

Place	Date	Hour	Summary of Events and Information	Remarks and references to Appendices
	Sept. 30.		Details shown strength of Bn. Reinforcement received during month. Side admission. Effective Strength	1 O.R. 1 officer 9 O.R. 10 officers 176 O.R.

Philip Eliard Major

APPENDIX A:

63rd M.G. Coy.

Firing Report

Date	Time	Position	Target	Rounds Fired	
Night of 31/1.Sept	3.15am	011a 02.45	—	2,000	Barrage to assist Brigade on our night who were making a Raid
1/2 Sept	10.0pm to 2.0am	014a 60.60	Roads leading from HOLLEBEKE CHATEAU	4000	
2/3	3pm to 3.15pm	02d 15.65	Aircraft	130	
	11.0pm to 4.0am	02d 15.65	Roads & tracks HOLLEBEKE CHATEAU necs 0.25 0030	600	
3/4	11.0pm to 4.0am	014a 60.60	Cross Roads & Roads leading from HOLLEBEKE CHATEAU	3000	
	7.30am	02d 15.60	Aircraft	1500	
4/5	5.0am	02d 15.65	Aircraft	62	
	10.0pm to 4.0am	014a 60.60	Track Junction i.Od.80.40	850	
5/6	11.0pm to 4.0am	014a 60.60	HOLLEBEKE CHATEAU Dugouts in Od Road	1500	
6/7				4500	Company Relieved

APPENDIX B

63 M. Gun Coy

DATE	TIME	GUN POSITION	TARGET	ROUNDS FIRED	REMARKS
29-9-14	1-15 am	J25a 6.3	J29c 35·80	625	
-do-	6-45 pm	J25b 15·62	J21d 49·19	5,500	on S.O.S Signal
-do-	at intervals	J25b 15·62	J24b 62·38	15,000	do
4th form to 29·9·14 8 pm to 9pm to 10/12 pm	4·5 pm to 5 pm		J24a 16·86		
30·9·14	10·3·0 pm to 3·30 pm	J25a J25b 60-30 J25b 34·46	J24b 6·8 J24b 62·38 J24b 15·06	4250 450 450	do Searched and traversed slightly
1-10-14	6·10 am	J25b·34·34 J25b·34·40 J25·b 34·44 J25·b 34·45 J25·b 34·63	Line from J21d 40 to J22c 04	1250 1000 1000 1100 115·5	Guns opened immediately S.O.S went and fired until the Artillery ceased
30·9·14	11·5 am to 1·15 am	J25b 34·44 J25·b 34·45		300 800	
30·9·14	6·45 pm	J25·b 34·34 J25·b 34·40 J25·b 34·44 J25·b 34·45 J25·b 34·53	J24d 40 to J25d 414	1100 1300 1250 1100 1250	Barrage from each gun traversing from left to right
30·9·14	9 pm to 12 mn	J25a·63 J24b·30	MARGATE FARM J24b 30.90	2000	

1-10-14

Bluffchival
Major

Commdg 63rd M. G Coy

4th Division

Herewith War Diary for
the Month of October 1917
Please acknowledge receipt
of same

63 Coy
Machine Gun Corps

War Diary
63rd M.G. Coy.
Oct 1917.

WAR DIARY or INTELLIGENCE SUMMARY

Army Form C. 2118.

(Erase heading not required.)

Place	Date	Hour	Summary of Events and Information	Remarks and references to Appendices
Mount Sorrel I 30 c 95.90.	Oct. 1		Our barrage positions were heavily shelled throughout the day. No casualties. Five bell boxes and oil cans blown up. The gun blown up on September 29 was replaced. Weather good. Firing as per appendix. A carrying party of 20 men was sent from rear H.Q. to take SAA to forwards and barrage positions	See appendix I "Firing Reports"
	" 2		Shelling still heavy on our barrage positions. No casualties. Weather good; bright sunshine. Firing as per appendix.	See App. I.
	" 3		Most of the day was spent preparing for the attack on the following day. A carrying party of 40 men was employed during morning & afternoon carrying SAA to all positions making each gun reserve up to 15000 rounds. Everything ready for new barrage by 6 p.m. Weather - rain in early a.m. Dull but fine afterwards. Casualties :— 2 men wounded. Firing as per appendix.	See App. I
	" 4		Zero day. Infantry 'zero' 6 a.m. 'Zero' for machine gunners 6.3 a.m. Heavy shelling all day. Two of No 1 Section's guns destroyed by shellfire. Also one of No 4 Section's. Firing as per appendix. Casualties Nil. Rain in early morning. Dull during the day. A new gun sent to No 1 Section by 5 p.m.	
	" 5		Barrage (5.15 a.m.) put down by our artillery. Shelling not so heavy as on previous day. Weather - High west wind. Showery all day. New gun sent to No 4 section. To "A" barrage positions 5 new barrels were sent and 6 to "B" barrage positions. Firing as per appendix. The following were sent up from rear H.Q. to replace casualties - 1 Sergeant & 4 other ranks	See App. I
	" 6	2.30 p.m	Relief orders received by 6th relieved by 19th G. Coy See Appendix.	See App. II "Relief Orders"
		9.15 p.m	Relief complete	
		11 p.m	5 officers and 100 men embussed at BUS HQ and proceeded to Rear HQ at BEAVER CAMP. Weather wet.	
BEAVER CAMP N 15 c 3.4 Sheet 28 S.W.	" 7		Rain all day. Men cleaning clothing and equipment.	
	" 8		Gun kit checked & cleaned. Also clothing & equipment. Company standing to. Weather wet.	
	" 9		Limbers packed and Company standing to.	
	" 10		Company bathed at Kennel. Company paid. One Officer reconnoitred prospective gun positions in J 19 d J 26 a and J 26 b (Shrewsbury Forest Map). See Appendix. 2 Lt. Johnston S taken on Coy strength.	See App. III Map "SHREWSBURY FOREST"

John Edward Major

WAR DIARY
or
INTELLIGENCE SUMMARY.
(Erase heading not required.)

Army Form C. 2118.

Place	Date	Hour	Summary of Events and Information	Remarks and references to Appendices
EDGE STREET TUNNELS	12	11.40	5.0 am 80 O.R. entrained at EE KLEM CORNER. Detrained at SPOILBANK. Relieved 112 H Coy at EDGE ST TUNNELS in sane dugout as III M.G. Coy. Guns placed as follows:— OC Battery at BODMIN COPSE J.19 d.45. Two guns of No 1 Section. 3 guns of No 2 Section. Under Lieut MACLEAN. (2) H Group in JAVA TRENCH J.26 a 3.5. Two guns under Lieut Dunning fire direct fire (3) I.4 J. 2 guns at J 30 b 80 30 & J 21 a 5.7. Two guns under 2 Lieut Jenkinson. (4) 2 Guns in reserve at MOUNT SORREL. Relief complete. Not subjected to undue shell fire. Day weather moderate. Visibility and available guides.	
	12	12 pm	Relief complete. Infantry H.Q. moved back to MOUNT SORREL. CANADA ST TUNNELS in afternoon. Casualties (killed 1 wounded). Fine morning wet evening. Att Jameson Sick & QCS.	
MOUNT SORREL	13		19 in 4 hour shoot in pattern at J 21 & J.25.90 S.A.A. carried by G.Bat. Weather fine	
	14		Activity of enemy by III M.G. Coy in nights J.15-16. III M.G. Coy officers visited line & taken over arrangements. Prisoners 3 killed 1 wounded. 3 left Farm. B. reports 11 Bdes III Coy for 58. Weather Showery. Relief fort fire officers to division order relieved by II. M.G. Coy. Weather Showery.	September 1 Hostility Caire
	15	3 pm	Place of officers & II. M.G. of the war. Final reconnoissance. All orders for information obtained as to pattern, orders for ODeM completed and in parts sent to D.H.Q. Carrier 9 members. 15 F + 8 OR went up from HQ & repre ourselves. Casualties. Evening 10 8 R were attacked...	
	16		III HC [Gunners?] in Stables at MOUNT SORREL at 3.30. H. + 4.30 repairing. Relay completed units hostility. Relay complete 9 pm. The day companies in 2 periods one at 6 pm 8 + 1 H + the other at BUS HQ. At 11 pm evening of FRONTIER CAMP 2 stage later. Weather good.	
FRONTIER CAMP	17		All Company present 8 am. until 8 pm. night CSH reported 12.30 p.m. Parable 10 am. Hour start for cleaning clothing equipment. Weather fine.	

[signature]

WAR DIARY
or
INTELLIGENCE SUMMARY.
(Erase heading not required.)

Army Form C. 2118.

Place	Date	Hour	Summary of Events and Information	Remarks and references to Appendices
FRONTIER CAMP	Oct. 18		Guns and ammunition cleaned and checked. Weather fair. CSM. Balkwell left Coy for U.K. to join H.E.	
	19		Coy bathed under Brigade arrangements, at ST JANS CAPPEL from 1 p.m. till 2.30 p.m.	
	20		Coy paraded for gun drill and later packed limbers preparatory to leaving camp. Weather still fair. 6 O.R. taken on strength as reinforcements.	
MERRIS	21		Coy marched from FRONTIER CAMP via BERTHEN & METEREN to billets at MERRIS arriving at 2 p.m. Weather fair.	
	22		Coy cleaning gun kit & equipment during morning. Sports in afternoon Football & Cross country running. Weather fair.	
	23		Coy cleaning gun kit & equipment & then carrying on with Training Programme. Recreational Training in afternoon. Weather fine.	For Training Programme See Appendix IV
	24		Coy carried on with Training Programme. In afternoon Sections 1.2 & 3. HQ staff & transport marched to OUTERSTEENE Baths F.8.a.90.40 (Belgium & Part of France 27 SE). Weather fine.	
	25		Training carried on as per programme. No 4 Section bathed at OUTERSTEENE between 8 & 9 a.m. Military medals awarded in B.R.O to Sgt Evans, Sgt Mitchell, L/Cpl Bond, Pte Jackson, & Pte Haywood for operations in SHREWSBURY FOREST on OCT. 4. 1917. Weather fair.	
	26		Coy carried out Training as per programme. Weather wet.	
	27		Coy parade until 10 a.m as per Programme of Training 12.15 p.m. Inspection by C.O. of Coy in Marching Order. Coy drill.	

WAR DIARY
or
INTELLIGENCE SUMMARY

Army Form C.2118.

Place	Date	Hour	Summary of Events and Information	Remarks and references to Appendices
MERRIS	28		Queue after parade inspection of 2nd Duke Cornwall's Staff sergeants Church Parade (C of E) at 3 p.m. in MERRIS school. Weather fine	
	29		Gy came on Defensive of trench. Fine weather. Left Bruk 6 pm H.E	
	30		Programme of training carried out. No 1 Section under special training for a section four.	
	31		Programme of training carried out. No 1 Section under special training for fault competition. 2nd Competition # 18 O.R. ready as reinforcements. Weather good	

NB The total number of parades fired by the Company's guns during the month & October was 166350.

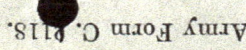

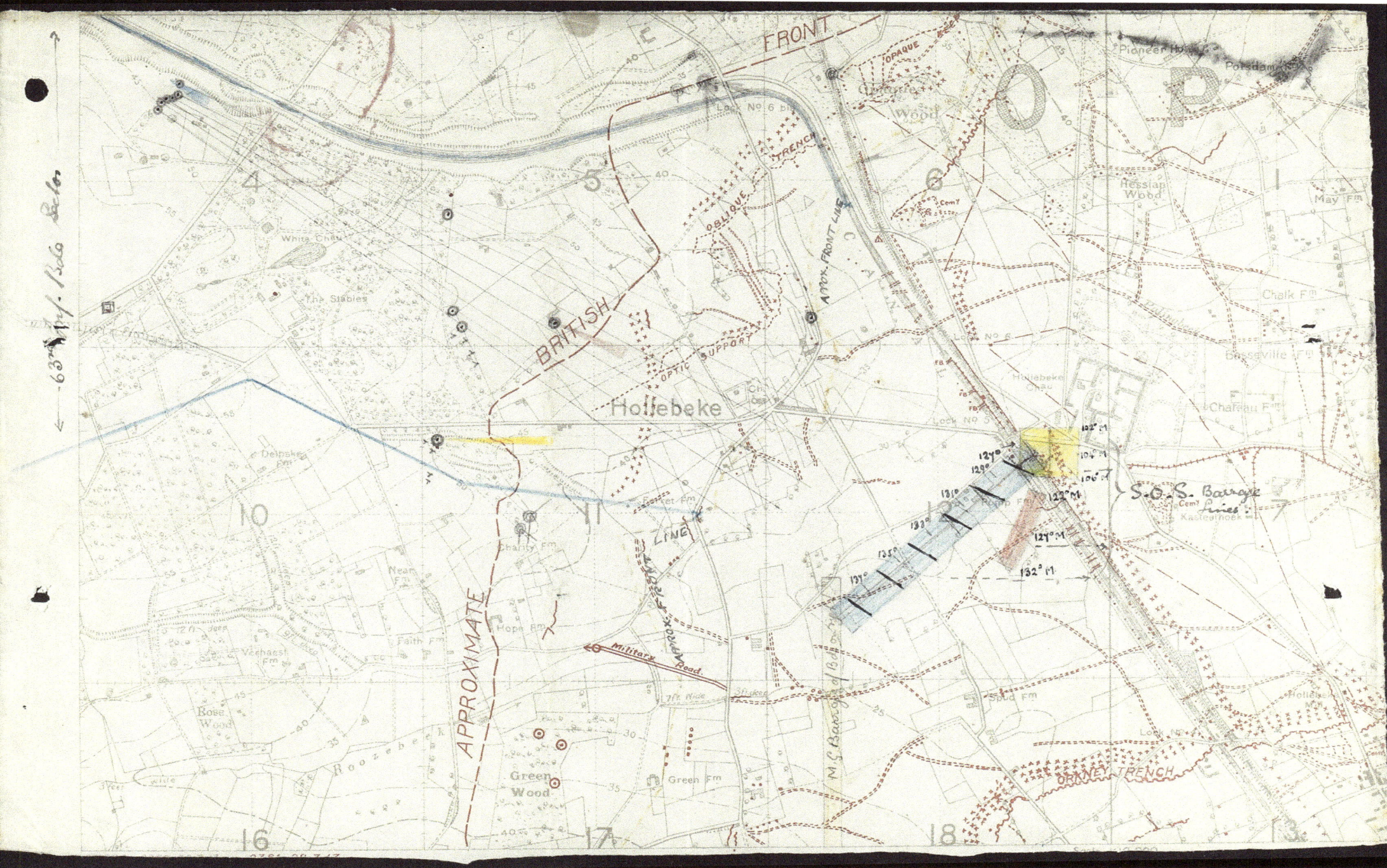

SHREWSBURY FOREST

German Trenches corrected to 10-9-17.

Part of Sheet 28.

No 2

MESSAGE MAP

SCALE 1/5,000.

September 1917.

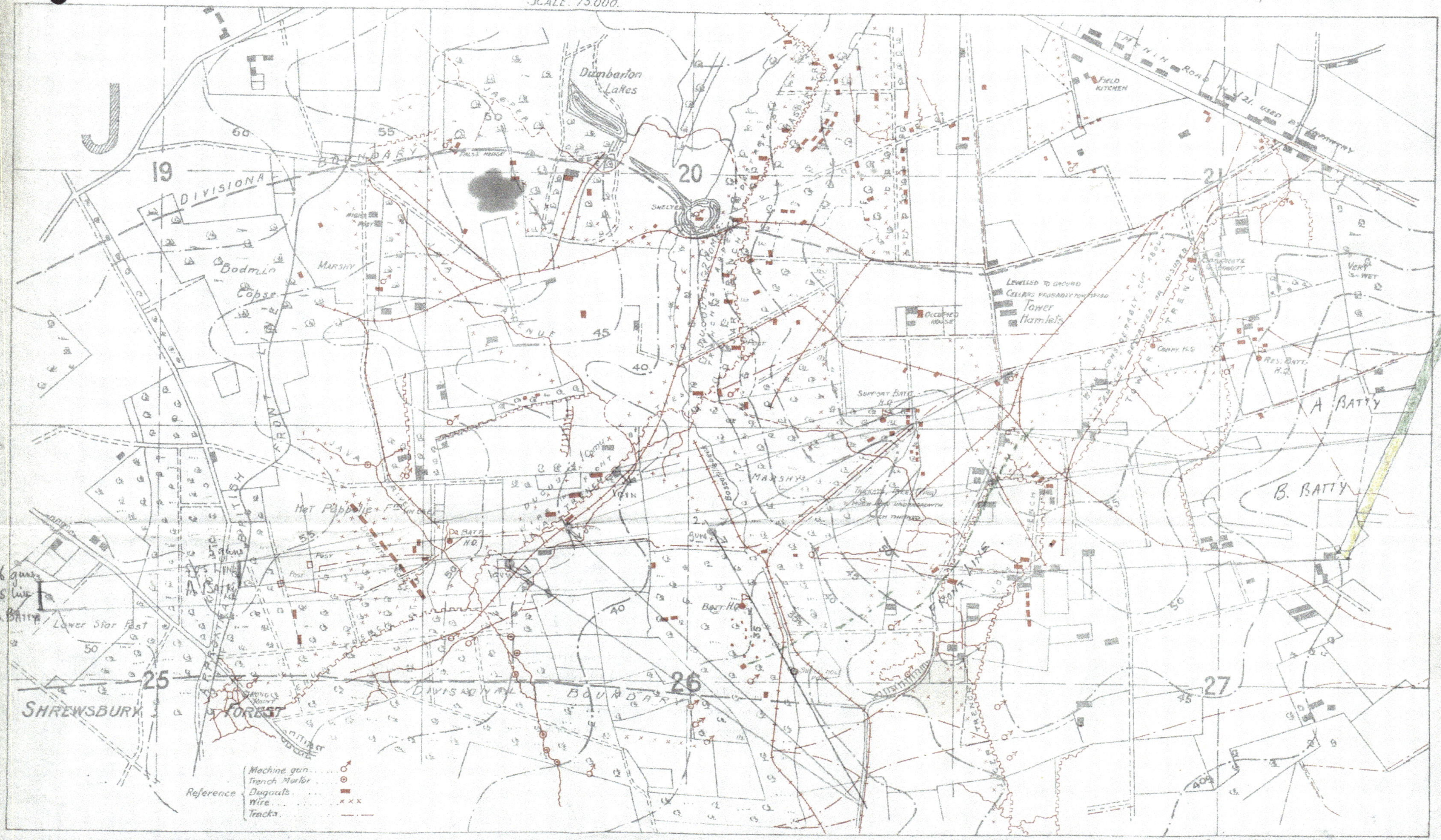

Printed by No 2 Advanced Section, A.P.&S.S. 12.9.17.

MESSAGE FORM

To:— 						No.

(Note:—Either give Map Reference or
1. I am at .... mark your position by a "X" on the
 (Map on back.
2. I have reached limits of my Objective.
3. My Platoon Company is at........................... and is consolidating.
4. My Platoon Company is at........................... and has consolidated.
5. Am held up by (a) M.G. (b) Wire at .... (Place where you are).
6. Enemy holding strong point...........................
7. I am in touch with .... on Right, Left, at ....
8. I am not in touch with .... on Right, Left.
9. Am shelled from...........................
10. Am in need of :—
11. Counter Attack forming at ....
12. Hostile (a) Battery (b) Machine Gun (c) Trench Mortar active at ....
13. Reinforcements wanted at........................... rifles.
14. I estimate my present strength at .... rifles.
15. Add any other useful information here:—

Name..............................
Platoon..............................
Time .... m.		Company..............................
Date .... 1917.		Battalion..............................

(A). Carry no maps or papers which may be of value to the Enemy.
(B). Give no information if captured, except the following, which
    you are bound to give:—
    Name, Rank, (Number) and Regiment.
(C). Collect all captured maps and papers and send them in at once.

63rd Machine Gun Coy
M.3

Appendix I

Firing Reports.

FIRING REPORT

No 1 SECTION

GUN POSITION	TIME & DATE	TARGET	No of ROUNDS	REMARKS
J25β 34-34	6.18 pm 1/10/17	S.O.S. Jai'd 40 to J30 40	1500 2000 2000 1450 1450	Rds 9000
J25β 34-40				
J25β 34-44				
J25β 34-48				
J25β 34-53				

Hurtchison
2/Lt Major
COMDG 63- GCoy

Bjør MacLim Lim Day

3

3rd Machine Gun Coy.

FIRING REPORT

No 1 SECTION

Gun Position	Time & Date	Target	No of Rounds	Remarks
J25 b 34.34 34.40 34.44 34.48 34.68	6-45 am 3/10/17	SOS Line J21d 70 J22 c 40	1750 1450 2000 1450 2500 total 9.750	

Ewett McMichael
Lieut

T. Weatherhead 2Lt for
Major
Commdg 63rd MG Coy

Firing Report

No 1 SECTION

GUN POSITION	TIME & DATE	TARGET No Rds	No OF ROUNDS	REMARKS
3458 3434	6.30 am	8.500	Once as shown in during	Damage put up as per order.
34.40	4-10-17	8.500		
34.44	do	9.020		Nos of fire ammunition
34.48	9.15 am	8.500	80 & five	elevated and howitzer
34.63	4-10-17	9.020		04 per order.
		HW 43.500		

Minimum

ATC .... MAJOR Commdg E&A "C" Coy

Officer Major Sein San Loy

3rd Machine Gun Coy.

FIRING REPORT   N.o 1 SECTION

Gun Position	Time & Date	Target	No of Rounds	Remarks
J26b.34.34	4 p.m.	S.O.S	1500	Fired when the S.O.S. went up
J26b.34.40	5.10.17.	Line	1400	on our Divisional Front. We were
J26b.34.44		J21d 4000	1500	heavily shelled while firing
J26b.34.48		to	1450	
J26 35 kl.		J22c.00.40.	1500.	
			Total 7350	

Philip C. Medcalf Lieut

W.H. Maclean 2/Lt. for O.C. N.o 1 Sect
for MAJOR
Commdg. 63rd M.G. Coy

DATE 6.10.17.

FIRING REPORT

No 4 SECTION

GUN POSITION	TIME & DATE	TARGET	No OF ROUNDS	REMARKS
J35o 6 from J37£	6.45 am to 6.20 am 1-10-17	from J.20.a.15. to J.20.d.15 Barrage	2000	New gun position

Officer McClure Lieu. 63rd Bay

Signed 63rd Bn. MAJOR
Comdg 63rd MGCoy

3rd Machine Gun Coy.

FIRING REPORT   N° 4 SECTION

IN POSITION	TIME & DATE	TARGET	NO OF ROUNDS	REMARKS
J 25 a	7-30 to 8 pm 1-10-17	J 27 c (Barrage	6.500	We were shelled most of the time with H.E & Shrapnel
J 25 a	8-15 to 9-30 pm -do-	-do-	7500	do

Total 14000

2/Lt. Major
Comdg 63rd G Coy

FIRING REPORT

No 4 SECTION

GUN POSITION	TIME & DATE	TARGET	No OF ROUNDS	REMARKS
7.25 a Guns 3&4	11/pm 2-10-14	Jayd 35.95' MAGATE FARM J25c.10.80 DUPLEX FARM	1000	
7.25 a all barrage guns	6.50 am to 6.30 am	7.34	1500 1500	All Westwood

Mitchell 2/Lt MAJOR
Comdg 63m GC 4

O.C. Mac Lem Gun Coy

3rd Machine Gun Coy.

4

FIRING REPORT

Nº 4 SECTION

Gun Position	Time & Date	Target	No of Rounds	Remarks
Barrage J25a	6.5 am to 9.30 " 4.10.17	J2y b J22 c J28 a J28 a c	38500	
J25 a	9.45 am 4.10.17	J27c 50.50	1000	
			total 39.500	

Edwin McClelland
m gun

B Walker
2/Lieut Major
Comdg O/C Coy

IN THE FIELD.
5-10-17

Particulars of "F" Major
63rd Machine Gun Company.

SECTION OFFICER _____

No 4 SECTION
63rd M.G.Coy.

Gun Position	Time & Date	Target	Rounds Expended	Remarks
J 25 a. 8 Guns	6pm 4-10-17	J 24 & J 34 & J 34 c	6.250	Harassing fire
J 25 a. H Guns	5.30am 5-10-17	-do-	1.020	[illegible] 13,250

SECTION OFFICER W. L. Maclean D/H   No. 4 SECTION

63rd M.G. Coy

Gun Position	Time & Date	Target	Rounds Expended	Remarks
J25a	6.50 P.M 5/10/17	J27b. J28a. J28c.	8,250	One gun out of action 5 guns firing
J25a	9.58 P.M "	"	6,250	" " " " "

Total 14,500

Men who were sent down for the new gun could not get to our position before 6 A.M 6/10/17 on account of the area J25a, being shelled.

In The Field
6/10/17

W. L. Maclean
Lieut
Commanding 63rd Machine Gun Coy

List No. 1 of Records Fixed During the Month
of October

168-350
166-350

APPENDIX No II

RELIEF ORDERS.

SECRET.

63rd Machine Gun Company
----

1. 63rd Machine Gun Company will be relieved as under tonight :-

2. (a) 112th Machine Gun Company will relieve-

   (i) 3 guns 63rd M.G.Coy. about J.26.a.6.8 and J.20.c.9.0.
   (ii) 2 guns   "   "   "   J.26.b.1.6 (to be relieved by 1 gun).

   (b) 19th Motor Machine Gun Battery (6 machine guns) will relieve -

   (i) 5 guns 63rd M.G.Coy. about J.25.b.3.4 (to be relieved by 3 guns)
   (ii) 6 guns   "   "   "   J.25.a.6.3 (to be relieved by 3 guns)

   and will come under command of G.O.C. 112th Inf. Bde.

3. 63rd Machine Gun Company will move to billets at BEAVER CAMP.

4. All details of relief will be arranged by officers commanding Machine Gun Companies and 19th Motor Machine Gun Battery.

5. Completion of relief will be reported to Headquarters 112th Infantry Brigade.

6. 10 busses for 63rd M.G.C. and 63rd T.M.B. will be at BUS HOUSE from 10 pm tonight, and will convey them to their respective billets.

   Officers will be sent down to BUS HOUSE at the above time to arrange about busses and to ensure that these are not taken by 111th M.G.C. and T.M.B. who are also being relieved.

6.10.17

Captain,
Brigade Major,
63rd Infantry Brigade.

SECRET.   Copy No. 13.

63rd Infantry Brigade Order No. 171.

October 13th 1917.

1. 63rd Infantry Brigade (less Machine Gun Company and T.M.Battery) will be relieved during night 14/15th October by 117th Infantry Brigade (less M.G. Company and T.M.Battery). Relief of 63rd M.G. Company and T.M.Battery will be carried out during night 15/16th October. 63rd M.G. Company will be relieved on 15th Oct. and during night 15/16th Oct., under arrangements to be made by D.M.G.O. Table of reliefs id attached.

2. No post or trench will be vacated until relieved.

3. All maps, plans, photographs, defence schemes, trench stores, details of work proposed or in hand, will be handed over to relieving units and receipts obtained.

4. On relief, units will be conveyed by bus to the MONT KOKEREELE Area and will occupy the same camps as formerly.

5. Advance billeting parties will be arranged for by the Staff Captain from rear Brigade H.Q. Details of lorry arrangements will be issued separately.

6. Relieving units are timed to arrive at J.28.a.8.5 as follows:-

   16th Sherwood Foresters   4.15 pm
   17th K.R.R.C.   4.45 pm
   17th Sherwood Foresters   5.15 pm
   16th Rifle Brigade   5.45 pm

   16th Rifle Brigade will be in reserve to 117th Inf. Bde. and will be accommodated as follows :-

   H.Q. and 2 companies   CANADA STREET TUNNELS.
   2 companies   HEDGE STREET TUNNELS.

7. Relief complete will be reported to Brigade Headquarters.

Issued at 5 pm.

                                        (signed)
                                        Captain,
                                        63rd Infantry Brigade.

Distribution.

War Diary G.S.File	1 - 3
Brigade Staff	4 - 8
8th Lincolns	9
8th Somersets	10
4th Middlesex	11
10th York & Lancs.	12
63rd M.G. Company	13
63rd T.M. Battery	14
Brigade Transport Officer	15
No. 2 Coy. Train	16
49th Field Ambulance	17
117th Inf. Bde.	18
111th " "	19
112th " "	20
D.M.G.O. " "	21
37th Division	22

63rd Infantry Brigade No. 2908.

TO ALL RECIPIENTS OF BRIGADE ORDER NO. 171.

All reliefs referred to in the above order have been postponed for 24 hours.

The same applies to Bus arrangements.

Also

In all cases in the above order and Bus arrangements, for the reference "J.23.a.3.5" read "J.23.a.3.5".

M.L.Winter..
Captain,
Brigade Major,
63rd Infantry Brigade.

13.10.17

SECRET.

63rd Infantry Brigade No. 29191

AMENDMENT NO.2 TO 63RD INF. BDE. ORDER NO. 171
DATED 13.10.17.
----

1. 63rd Infantry Brigade will be relieved by 116th Inf. Bde. and not by 117th Inf. Bde.

2. In the above order, where

   "16th Sherwood Foresters" occurs read "14th Hants. Regt."
   "17th K.R.R.C."   "   "   "12th Sussex Regt."
   "17th Sherwood Foresters"   "   "   "13th Sussex Regt."
   "16th Rifle Brigade"   "   "   "11th Sussex Regt."

   and for "117th M.G.Company" and "117th T.M.Battery" read "116th M.G.Company" and "116th T.M.Battery".

3. On table issued with above order,
   Line 1, "Remarks Column", delete from "16th Sherwood Foresters" down to "Into the line."

4. Acknowledge.

W.P.Sterin(?)
Captain,
Brigade Major,
63rd Infantry Brigade.

14.10.17

To all recipients of 63rd Inf. Bde. Order 171 except 117th Inf. Bde.

APPENDIX

No 3

MAP

APPENDIX IV

Training Programme.   from 24-10-17
                       to   31-10-17.

Programme of Training 21-10-17 to 27-10-17.

Date	Time	Unit	Description of Training	Locality	Remarks
Saturday 24-10-17	8AM to 9AM	63rd M.G.Coy	Infantry Drill	(a) Parade Ground	
	9AM to 10AM	"	Mechanism & Immediate Action, Points before, during & after firing & to be brought out.	(a) Parade Ground	
	10AM to 1.30PM	"	No. 4 Section on Range.		
	10AM to 10.45AM	"	Lecture on Overhead Fire, It's uses. Collection (of) Ground on Tuesdays Lecture.		
	11AM to 1.30PM	"	Rough Ground Drill. No. 1, 2 Sections / No. 3 Section Pack Transport / Football, Cross Country Running		
	Afternoon				
Thursday 25-10-17	8AM to 9AM	"	Infantry Drill	(a) Parade Ground	
	9AM to 10AM	"	Mechanism & Immediate Action, Points before, during & after firing to be brought out.	(a) Parade Ground	
	10AM to 1.30PM	"	No. 1 Section on Range		
	10AM to 10.45AM	"	Lecture on Indirect Fire, Collision or Defilade (on) Parade Ground Lecture.		
	11AM to 1.30PM	"	Rough Ground Drill. No. 2, 3 Sections Limber / No. 4 Section Pack Transport / Football, Cross Country Running		
	Afternoon				

Programme of Work 21.10.17 to 27.10.17.

Date	Time	Unit	Description of Training	Locality	Remarks
Friday 26.10.17	8AM to 9AM	63rd M.G Coy	Infantry Drill.	Coy Parade Ground	
	9AM to 10AM	"	Mechanism & Immediate Action. Points before, during & after firing to be brought out.	Coy Parade Ground	
	10AM to 1.30PM	"	No 2 Section on Range	F 21 a 9.7.	
	10AM to 10.45AM	"	Lecture on "Barrage Fire"	Coy Parade Ground	
	11 to 1.30PM	"	Rough Ground Drill		
			Nos 1 & 4 Sections Pack Transport Limbers	X 25 d	
			No 3 Section Pack Transport	X 26 a	
	Afternoon	"	Football & Cross Country Running.		
Saturday 27.10.17	8AM to 9AM	63rd M.G Coy	Infantry Drill.	Coy Parade Ground	
	9AM to 10AM	"	Mechanism & Immediate Action. Points before, during & after firing to be brought out	Coy Parade Ground	
	10AM to 1.30PM	"	No 3 Section on Range	F 21 a 9.7	
	10AM to 10.45AM	"	Lecture on Reconnaissance required by Machine Gunners for Trench Warfare & for Open fighting.	Coy Parade Ground	
	11AM to 1.30PM	"	Rough Ground Drill		
			Nos 1 & 2 Pack Limbers	X 25 d	
			No 4 Section Pack Transport	X 26 a	
	Afternoon	"	Football & Cross Country Running		

Robert McNeal
Capt.

Programme of Training from 28.10.17 to 3.11.17

Date	Time	Unit	Description of Training	Locality	Remarks
Monday 29.10.17	8AM to 9AM 9AM to 9.45AM 10AM to 11AM 11AM to 1.30PM	63rd Machine Gun Company	Mechanism & Immediate Action (Blindfolded) Lecture, Lubrication & examination of the arm after the nights firing Gallery Drill Rough Ground Drill No 2 Section on Range.	Coy Billet Coy Parade Ground X334 426a F31 a.9.7	Afternoon Football.
Tuesday 30.10.17	8AM to 9AM 9AM to 9.45AM 10AM to 11AM 11AM to 1.30PM		Stripping the Lock & Gun (Blindfolded) Lecture on Military Geography Gallery Drill Rough Ground Drill No 3 Section on Range.	Coy Billet Coy Parade Ground X334 426a F31 a.9.7	Afternoon Football.
Wednesday 31.10.17	8AM to 9AM 9AM to 9.45AM 9AM to 11AM 11AM to 12AM 12NN to 1.30PM		Mechanism Immediate Action Drill before during & after firing & the thought out. Lecture on Repair Machine Gallery Drill Elementary Gun Drill Judging distance & using the Range Finder.	Coy Billet Coy Parade Ground Coy Parade Ground Coy Parade Ground	Football.

H Ashland Lieut

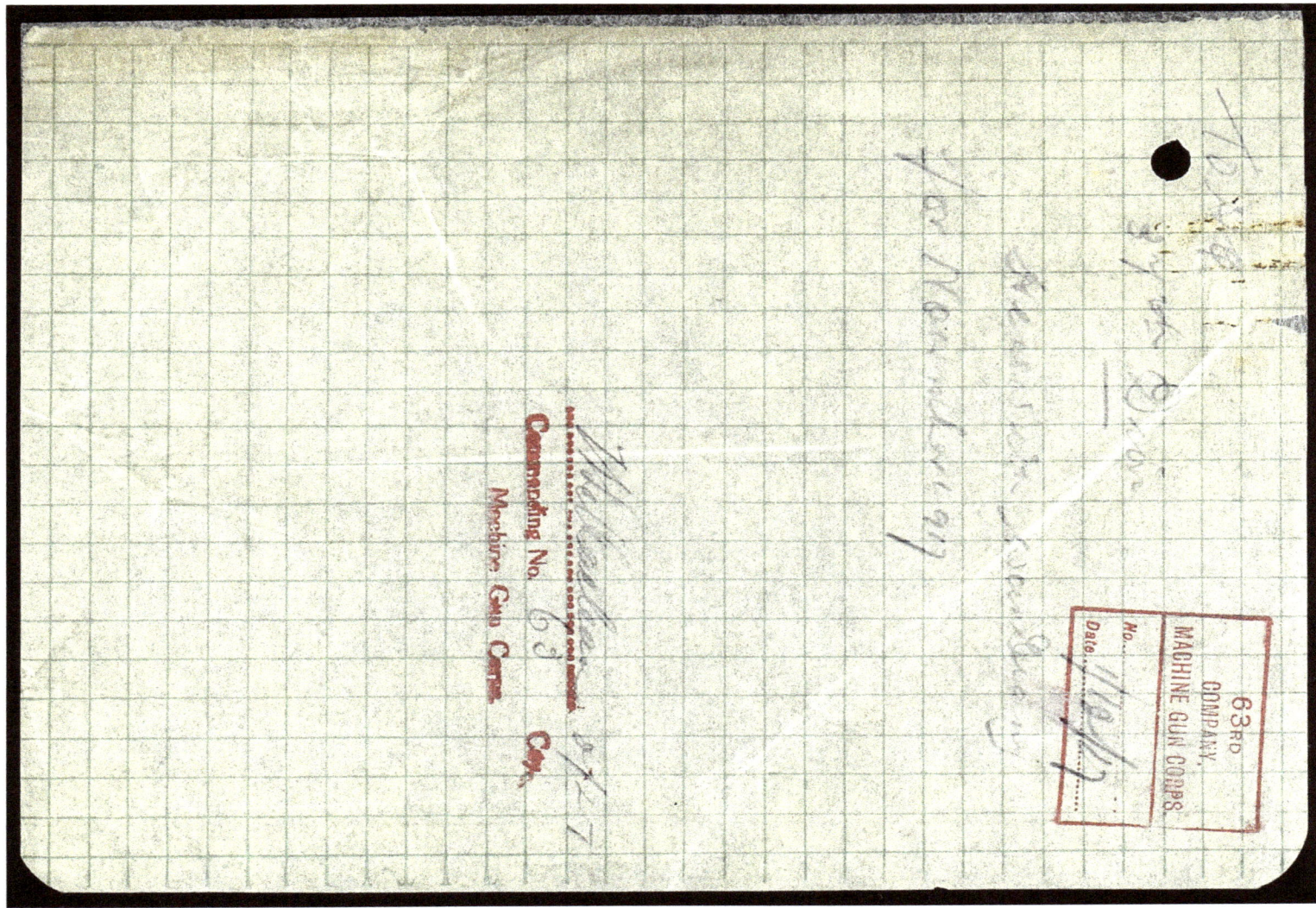

WAR DIARY
or
INTELLIGENCE SUMMARY.
(Erase heading not required.)

Instructions regarding War Diaries and Intelligence Summaries are contained in F. S. Regs., Par. II. and the Staff Manual respectively. Title pages will be prepared in manuscript.

63RD COMPANY. MACHINE GUN CORPS.

No ....
Date 1·12·17

Army Form C. 2118.

Place	Date	Hour	Summary of Events and Information	Remarks and references to Appendices
	1917			
Merris	Nov 1		Coy Training – Mech & I.A. Gun & Infantry Drill – carried out. No 1 Section practising for Divl Competition along with their Transport. Demonstration by NCO's in use of Yukon Pack. Weather Dull.	See Appendix 1.
Merris	Nov 2		Training carried out as on Nov 1, with lecture on Conventional Signs. Yukon Pack practice. Coy was paid. Weather very dull	
Merris	Nov 3		Coy Training carried out, Infantry Drill, I.A. Kit Inspection. G.O.C 63rd Inf Bde. inspected the Company Transport at 10·30 am. Afternoon, football match Transport v Sections was played. Weather still dull.	
Merris	Nov 4		Sunday. Inspection & fitting of Equipment. R.C & C of E Church Parades. Afternoon – football & in the evening a concert was held in the mens billets. Weather was dull but dry	
Merris	Nov 5		Training programme carried on. 2 Sections on Range, remainder Infantry & Gun Drill with lecture – MG's in attack. Football match at W 17 d·3·8 between Coy & 111th MG Coy. Fine weather.	

A6945 Wt. W11422/M1160 350,000 12/16 D. D. & L. Forms/C./2118/14.

Army Form C. 2118.

WAR DIARY
or
INTELLIGENCE SUMMARY.

(Erase heading not required.)

Instructions regarding War Diaries and Intelligence
Summaries are contained in F. S. Regs., Part II.
and the Staff Manual respectively. Title pages
will be prepared in manuscript.

Commanding No. 63 Machine Gun Corps.

A6945 Wt.W1142/M1160 350,000 12/16 D.&L. Forms/C./2118/14.

Place	Date	Hour	Summary of Events and Information	Remarks and references to Appendices
	1917			
Meaus	Nov 6		Coy bathed at Outbestere + afterwards paraded for cleaning guns. Insp reading etc. Officers spent morning on Bombs, Lewis gun, Vickers gun etc. reconnoitred line	
Meaus	Nov 7		with O.M.G. + in evening left Coy to be temporarily attached to Bde H.Q. 2nd Lt Newsom – C.O. Lt Banning 2nd in command. Weather dull + raining. Rain interrupted training programme in morning. Reorganised Bde + section No 2 Section on Range. One section of transport used for first transport competition at X.22. c.4.5. Weather fine in afternoon + fatigue match was played.	
Meaus	Nov 8		11 Banning reconnoitred Gun positions in the line. Training programme carried out. Guns cleaned. Specialists classes P.T. Semaphore shop reading Vickers guns and Lewis gun	
Nov 9	Nov 9		Company left Meaus 9:30 am for York Huts (Bois Ricca) N.23.c arrived 1PM. Route via Boirieux. Fine weather. No stragglers	
Nov 10	Nov 10		Company left York Huts (N.23.c) for Camp at No 2 Kemp Reservoir arrived about 12:30 PM. Very wet weather. Camp in rather state. Mud up to knees. Men in huts. Limbers in the open. Took over from 52nd M.G. Coy.	

WAR DIARY
or
INTELLIGENCE SUMMARY.
(Erase heading not required.)

Army Form C. 2118.

Instructions regarding War Diaries and Intelligence Summaries are contained in F. S. Regs., Part II. and the Staff Manual respectively. Title pages will be prepared in manuscript.

Place	Date	Hour	Summary of Events and Information	Remarks and references to Appendices
	1917			
N 10 a.	Nov 11		Sunday. 8 teams of Nos 1 + 2 Sections left Camp for the Line about 1.30 PM	
Adv Coy			Remainder of Company worked on drainage. Nothing special to report.	
HQ			Weather very wet again.	
SPOILBANK			In the line Sections 1 + 2 relieved 8 teams of No 247 Coy to front and right	
I 33.d.40.60.			front of Fusilier Wood. Guns Nos 3, 4, 5, 6 taken over by No 1 Section, Nos 9, 10, 15, 16	
REAR HQ			by No 2 Section. Map Refs below. See Map appended. Relief complete 6.45 pm.	
ESSEX CAMP			Guns 15 + 16 fired as per Appendix No 2. Weather fair, some showers.	
N 21. a. 1.9			MAP. REFS. OF GUNS	
			Sect HQ	GUNS	GUNS
			No 1 O 6. a. 4. 8	No 5 O.6.c.4.8.	No 9 J 31c. 00. 65	
			No 2 I 36.c.6.7	No 6 O.6.c.65.90	No 10 J 31c. 2. 2	
				No 7 O.6.b.90. 35	No 15 I 36.c. 60. 85.	
				No 8 P. 1. a. 0. 4	No 16 I 36.c. 60. 85.	

A6945 Wt. W11422/M1160 350,000 12/16 D. D. & L. Forms/C./2118/14.

Commanding No. 63 Coy
Machine Gun Corps.

WAR DIARY or INTELLIGENCE SUMMARY.

(Erase heading not required.)

Army Form C. 2118.

Instructions regarding War Diaries and Intelligence Summaries are contained in F. S. Regs., Part II. and the Staff Manual respectively. Title pages will be prepared in manuscript.

Place	Date	Hour	Summary of Events and Information	Remarks and references to Appendices
	1917 Nov 12		The day was quiet and routine work was carried out. Firing as per appendix no 3. Camp at N.10.a vacated at 10 am, the Sections out of the line and Transport moved to BEDFORD CAMP N21.a.2.3. arrived about noon, Coy in Huts and animals under cover. Unable to hand over the Camp at N.10.A, did not find Area Commandant until Tuesday 13th Nov. Weather fine.	
	Nov 13		Teams in the line busy improving positions and accomodation. Casualties - Nil. Firing as per appendix no 4. Weather fine. Sections out of the line carried out training programme - Mechanism Inspection, Squad Drill, Limber cleaning etc. No 6 Sub area Commandant handed receipt for area Stores which were brought from N.10.a. Sent his NCO to inspect the Camp.	
	Nov 14		Routine work of improving and cleaning up Gun positions carried on. Firing as per appendix no. 5. Casualties - Nil. Dull weather. Training carried out by Sections out of the line consisted of - P.T. Mechanism + I.A. Gas Drill etc. Somerset's Transport played our Transport at football MGC came out second best.	

Commanding No 63 Coy
Machine Gun Corps.

WAR DIARY
or
INTELLIGENCE SUMMARY.
(Erase heading not required.)

Army Form C. 2118.

Instructions regarding War Diaries and Intelligence Summaries are contained in F. S. Regs., Part II. and the Staff Manual respectively. Title pages will be prepared in manuscript.

Place	Date	Hour	Summary of Events and Information	Remarks and references to Appendices
	1917			
	Nov 15		Work at Gun positions carried on. Six men sent to No I Section to assist. Firing as per appendix No 6. Casualties – NIL. Bright weather. Sections out of the line carried out training programme – P.T. Mechanism + I.A. Squad + arm Drill, Revolver Drill. 2nd Lt Forrest + 3 Signallers proceeded to CURRAGH CAMP (Canada Corner M 17 c) to take over. 3 Signallers left in charge.	
	Nov 16		Work in the line carried on. Casualties – NIL. Firing as per appendix No 7. Usual training and limber cleaning done by Sections out of the line. Operation orders received for move to new Camp.	
	Nov 17		Quiet day. Work continued. Casualties – NIL. 2 men sick. Firing as per appendix No 8. Weather misty. Move to CURRAGH CAMP (Canada Corner M 17 c) cancelled. 2nd Lt Maclean + Sgt Evans went into the line. Training programme carried out by Sections not in the line.	

A6945   Wt. W11422/M1160   350,000   12/16   D. D. & L.   Forms/C./2118/14.

Commanding No 63
Machine Gun Corps.

WAR DIARY or INTELLIGENCE SUMMARY

Army Form C. 2118.

Place	Date	Hour	Summary of Events and Information	Remarks and references to Appendices
	1917 Nov 18		Teams in the line relieved. Relief completed by 6 PM. Quiet all day. Casualties – NIL. Firing as per appendix no Dull weather. Nos 3 & 4 Sections left Camp at 1pm in lorries and relieved Nos 1 & 2 Sections in the line. Cpl Wray + 3 Signallers relieved Signallers of No 247 Coy. Relieved Sections arrived at BEDFORD CAMP N21.a.1.9. at 7.30 PM.	
	Nov 19		Very quiet all day. Teams in the line busy improving and making shelters, drainage etc. Casualties – NIL. Firing as per appendix no 9. Transport & Details moved from BEDFORD CAMP N21.a.1.9 to ESSEX CAMP N21.a.1.9 at 10.30 am. Men who had come from the line were busy cleaning up. Weather fair.	
	Nov 20		Enemy shelled round IMPERIAL DUGOUTS during the night. Ration party also shelled from RAILWAY DUMP to IMPERIAL DUGOUTS. Work in the line done as appendix no 10. Firing as per appendix no Casualties – NIL. Dull weather. Sections out of the line paraded for inspection. Special inspection of attached men.	

WAR DIARY
or
INTELLIGENCE SUMMARY.
(Erase heading not required.)

Instructions regarding War Diaries and Intelligence Summaries are contained in F. S. Regs., Par. II. and the Staff Manual respectively. Title pages will be prepared in manuscript.

Army Form C. 2118.

Place	Date	Hour	Summary of Events and Information	Remarks and references to Appendices
	1917			
	Nov 21		Very quiet all day. A little busy around RAILWAY DUMP. Teams in the line busy making and improving emplacements and Dugouts. Casualties – 1 Sick. Firing as per appendix no. 11 Dull weather. Sections out of the line, and Transport bathed at CONFUSION CORNER N 10. b. Private Bruce remanded for F.G.C.M. absent without leave.	
	Nov 22		Enemy shelled J 31 C 00 65. at 4.30 Am with 4.2's ten rounds and gas shells intermittently throughout the night. Teams in the line busy making emplacements. Casualties – 1 wounded. Firing as per appendix no. 12 Good weather. Training carried on for teams out of the line + football in the afternoon. Lt Denning went to Hospital. Lt Thomson 2nd in command.	
	Nov 23		Teams in the line busy making and improving emplacements + dugouts. Filling Belts. Examination of Ammunition, Rifles + Revolvers. Firing as per appendix no 13 No 9 Gun moved into dugout which fires through loophole. Enemy sent 2 shells – 4.2 – on 200 x NE of No 9 Gun at 7.15 Am Casualties – NIL. Training programme carried out for Sections out of the line. Sgt Mitchell. J.W. to 220 Coy as C.Q.M.S.	

A6945 Wt. W11422/M1160 350,000 12/16 D. D. & L. Forms/C./2118/14.

Commanding No. 65 Coy.

Machine Gun Corps.

WAR DIARY
or
INTELLIGENCE SUMMARY.
(Erase heading not required.)

Army Form C. 2118.

Place	Date	Hour	Summary of Events and Information	Remarks and references to Appendices
	1917			
	Nov 24		Teams in the line making Latrines, building emplacements, and Flash Protectors. Enemy shelled the BLUFF with Gas and BATTLE WOOD with 5.9s or 4.2's. Casualties – NIL. Firing as per appendix 14. Sections out of the line – Kit Inspection, Tactical Exercise & preparation for the line. 2nd Lt Thornton went to Field Ambulance. CSM Sykes reported for Duty.	
	Nov 25		Teams in the line busy making & improving emplacements and Dugouts and fitting same with Gas Blankets. Transport Corner shelled with 5.9, 4.2, 9.2. Enemy Aeroplanes bombing back areas at night. Firing as per appendix No 15. Casualties – NIL. Nos 1 & 2 Sections relieved 3 & 4. Relief completed 4:30 PM. CSM Sykes took charge of No 1 Section Guns. Sections went up in trains and relieved Sections returned in busses. Weather fair.	
	Nov 26		Teams in the line making Latrines etc. Enemy very quiet. Firing as per appendix No 16. Casualties NIL. Sections out of the line resting and cleaning up. Weather Dull.	

No 63 Machine Gun Corps

WAR DIARY
INTELLIGENCE SUMMARY
(Erase heading not required.)

Army Form C. 2118.

Place	Date	Hour	Summary of Events and Information	Remarks and references to Appendices
	1917 Nov 26 (contd)		In the line. — At 3.30 pm 2nd Lt Shoesmith O.C. MAT was relieved at Coy HQrs by 2 Lt Mawson MAT and at 6 pm Sgt Major Sykes was relieved by Sgt Syme at Section HQrs Nos 5, 6, 7, & 8 guns. Nos 15 & 16 guns fired as per fixing report during night 26/27 Nov 1917.	
	Nov 27		10 day arrangements have been made with O.C. Canadian Smoothing Company to put a dump in the tunnel Emplacements of O.C. 65.90. This is necessary to keep the emplacement dry. The work will be commenced tomorrow 28/11/17. Firing as per appendix No 17.	
			Sections out of the line carried out training programmes, inspection of rifles equipment Respirator Belt etc. Weather fine.	
	Nov 28		Situation unchanged. No 7 gun position at No 1 gun fired from further around during the night. Firing as per appendix No 18. In camp, programme of training was carried out. Instruction + A Lesson, Indoor drill, Recognition. Weather fine.	

WAR DIARY or INTELLIGENCE SUMMARY

Army Form C. 2118.

(Erase heading not required.)

Place	Date	Hour	Summary of Events and Information	Remarks and references to Appendices
	1917 Nov 29		Situation unchanged. Casualties - NIL. Firing report as per appendix No 19. Weather fair. Sections out of the line carried out training programme including tactical exercise.	
	Nov 30		Situation unchanged. Casualties - 3. (slightly wounded) Firing as per appendix No 20. Sections in Camp. Gun cleaning and preparation for the line. Weather was fine.	

APPENDIX I

Programme of training 29.10.17 to 3.11.17

Date	Hour	Description of training	Locality	Remarks
Thursday 1.11.17	8AM to 9AM	Mechanism and Immediate action. Faults before during + after firing to be thought out.	Coy Billets	
	9AM to 9.45	Lecture on Anti Aircraft	Coy Billets	
	10AM to 11AM	Infantry Drill	Coy Parade Ground	
	11AM to 12AM	Stationary Gun Drill	Coy Parade Ground	
	12AM to 1.30PM	Judging distance + using the Range finder	Coy Parade Ground	
	afternoon	football		
Friday 2.11.17	8AM to 9AM	Mechanism + Immediate action. Faults before during + after firing to be thought out.	Coy Billets	
	9AM to 9.45	Lecture on continuous sighs	Coy Billets	
	10AM to 11AM	Infantry Drill		
	11AM to 1.30PM	Rough Ground Drill	Coy Parade Ground	X25d x26A
	afternoon	football		
Saturday 3.11.17	8AM to 9AM	Mechanism + Immediate action. Faults before during + after firing to be thought out.	Coy Billets	
	9AM to 11AM	Cleaning up for kit Inspection	Coy Billets	
	11AM to 1.30PM	Inspection + Infantry Drill	Coy Parade Ground	W.Hetherton Lt
	afternoon	football		

Details of Gun Positions.

Checked 13/11/17.

Gun No	Map Ref	Mag. Bearing	Traverse	Approachable by Day	Observe Enemy Movements	Field of Fire	Whether Shelled by Enemy	Ways of Approach	Accommodation	Whether under Observation by Enemy	Any Aircraft Mounting
3	O.6.c 7.8.	138°	15° L 10° R	Movement in Daytime is Unwise			No	By C.T. halfway from Section H.Q. Then along Embankment. Believed to be under observation.	Open Emplacement. Weatherproof Dugout Under Construction for 3 Gun	Approach is Believed to be But not the Emplacements.	No
4	O.6.c 65.90.	123°	15° L 17° R				No.				No
5	O.6.b 90.35.	174° 30'	24° L 32° R	No			Yes Slightly But 100' to Right.	By Trench & Duckboard Track. Under Observation from Right & Front.	No	Yes.	No
6	P.1.a O.4.	122° 30'	30° L 30° R	No					No		No
9	J.31.c 00.65.	103° 30'		Able to See Tracks Leading to Enemy Infantry Posts.	Right 1000' Front 400' Left 400'			Good Dugout	Yes	No
10	J.31.c 18.20.	148° 30'			Right 500' Front 700' Left 400'	Yes Intermittently		Good Dugout.	Yes	No
15	I.36.c 60.85.	138°	6° R	Yes			No		Good Dugout		No
16	I.36.c 60.85.	150°	6° L	Yes.			No		Good Dugout.		No

W. Maclean 2/Lt

WAR DIARY
or
INTELLIGENCE SUMMARY.
(Erase heading not required.)

Army Form C. 2118.

63 M.G. Coy

Place	Date	Hour	Summary of Events and Information	Remarks and references to Appendices
LINE	1921			
	May 1		In the line. Things were fairly quiet all day. No guns were located and Section HQ has been preceding satisfactorily at all gun positions with work. Faubus at No 5 gun a very much better since the swamp was put on. The pump is working well. The MGO visited coy HQ at 12.45 pm. Casualties - Nil. Firing as per appendix No 1. Sections in camp were preparing for the line cleaning guns kit etc. A very wet day.	
B822			Enemy visited I 36 d 98-65 BATTLE WOOD, FUSILIER WOOD + RAILWAY EMBANKMENT with 10 Rounds - Snow Gates - Bridge was built over Shell hole in duckboard track near Section HQs IMPERIAL DUGOUTS. SAA carried to positions. Sanitary fatigues. Fired outside day and for 12 Guns. Casualties - Nil - Firing as per appendix No 2.	
			Jnrs 3 & 4 Sections left Essex CAMP at 12.30 pm to entrain at SCHOOL HOUSE SIDING (N 21 a T 5) 1.15 pm for STOCKBANK to relieve Jnrs 1 + 2. Sections in the Line. Another four.	

A6945 Wt. W11423/M1160 350,000 12/16 D.D. & L. Forms/C./2118/14.

WAR DIARY
or
INTELLIGENCE SUMMARY.
(Erase heading not required.)

Army Form C. 2118.

Place	Date	Hour	Summary of Events and Information	Remarks and references to Appendices
	1917			
	Dec 3		Enemy shelled Nos 7 & 8 Guns about six shells of small calibre, also Nos 9 & 15 Gun Positions with Gas Shells, and OAF AVENUE. Enemy machine gun fired over IMPERIAL DUGOUTS. A Dugout was arranged for the Canteen and new Flash Protectors made for each gun. No 9 Gun moved inside Dugout. No 5 position was pumped. All arm & gas appliances were inspected by Section officers. Casualties - NIL. Firing as per appendix No 3. Sections out of the line were at the disposal of Section officers for cleaning up etc. Weather was good - cold and frosty.	
	Dec 4		No 15 Gun was shelled by the enemy at 4.30 pm but not hit. H.2's were used on OAF AVENUE & TRANSPORT CORNER by the Enemy. We helped the R E's with dugout for the Canteen near Section H.Q. and Latrine made at No 7 Gun. Casualties - NIL. Firing as per Appendix No 4. Half Company out of the line was inspected by O.C. and training carried out as per programme. Weather cold & frosty.	4

WAR DIARY
or
INTELLIGENCE SUMMARY

Army Form C. 2118.

Place	Date	Hour	Summary of Events and Information	Remarks and references to Appendices
	1917			
	Aug 5		Rather quiet throughout the day on the line only a few shots were exchanged by the enemy in the RAVINE in the afternoon. Casualties – Nil. Weather fairly good. Enemy Guns as per opinions on S.A.A. was carried, dugout cleared of water, new trench protector made for H.Q. Guns. No 5 position was bombed. Company moved to BAROSSA CAMP. Left ESSEX CAMP at 1.30 pm, move completed at 3.10 pm. Transport lines also at ESSEX CAMP.	
	Aug 6		Enemy was more active to-day and shelled No 3 Section H.Q. with H.E. OAK AVENUE was also shelled. Enemy M.Gs were active against our front. Casualties – Nil. Firing as far as appears to be Section on of the line consists on training programme, and Lt Stevenson, Sgt Barry, Lance Nuttall proceeded to CAMIERS. 2nd Lt HD Orton reported to Company for duty.	

WAR DIARY or INTELLIGENCE SUMMARY

Army Form C. 2118.

(Erase heading not required.)

Place	Date	Hour	Summary of Events and Information	Remarks and references to Appendices
	1917 Dec 7		A quiet day in the line. Enemy sent 4 shells into OAF AVENUE. Enemy MG's were very active against our aircraft. Casualties – NIL. Firing as per appendix no 7. Weather fair. 6000 SAA carried from Dump to Section HQ. Duckboards were repaired over shell holes. New Flash Protector made for No 16 Gun, and the ammunition in belts was turned. For Sections out of the line – Kit inspection, Baths, + usual parades. Sgt Cutler returned from Course. 4 Reinforcements from Base.	
	Dec 8		Enemy shelled No 10 Position from 3.10 pm to 4.30 pm with 6" + 9.2 and 19 smaller ones from direction ZANDVOORDE. Our aircraft was very active during the day. Mr Faulkner visited N. Lancs. and E Lancs Brigade HQ's. Casualties – NIL. Weather fair with some rain at night. Firing as per appendix no. 8. No 10 dugout cleared up after shelling. 14000 SAA carried. Sections out of the line carried out training programme.	

WAR DIARY
or
INTELLIGENCE SUMMARY.
(Erase heading not required.)

Instructions regarding War Diaries and Intelligence Summaries are contained in F. S. Regs., Part II. and the Staff Manual respectively. Title pages will be prepared in manuscript.

Army Form C. 2118.

Place	Date	Hour	Summary of Events and Information	Remarks and references to Appendices
	1917 Dec 9		Nos 1 & 2 Sections relieved 3 & 4 in the line. Relief complete 5pm. Enemy shelled FUSILIER WOOD with 30 rounds 4.2 from an Easterly direction. Casualties – NIL. Sections cleaned up generally all day. Work at No 10 Position was carried on. Firing as per appendix No 9 Details of Nos 3 & 4 Sections left BAROSSA CAMP for RIDGEWOOD at 2pm. where the Sections out of the line are to form a working party under C.R.E. 37th Div. Weather was bad.	
	Dec 10		Enemy was very active to day. A Patrol bombed our posts near 0.6.d.2.5. His artillery was active on OAK AVENUE in the morning. (5.9's were used). and also on 0.5.C.2.9. Light field on north side of BATTLE WOOD. all fired from south of ZANDVOORDE T.M. sent three shots at once on 0.6.d.7.9. Casualties – NIL. Weather dull & cloudy, clearing about noon. Firing as per appendix No 10. Gun Positions drained & trench built up. Tunnel pumped dry & cleaned. 12000 Rounds SAA carried to No 16 Position. Work at No 10 Gun completed.	

A6945 Wt. W11422/M1160 350,000 12/16 D. D. & L. Forms/C./2118/14.

WAR DIARY or INTELLIGENCE SUMMARY.

(Erase heading not required.)

Army Form C. 2118.

Place	Date	Hour	Summary of Events and Information	Remarks and references to Appendices
	1917 Dec 10 (cont'd)		Inspections were carried out as per routine. Nos 3 & 4 Sections were on working party under C.R.E all day at TOURNAY CAMP. They had baths in the evening at CONFUSION CORNER.	
	Dec 11		A quiet day in the line, no shelling near the Gun Positions. Casualties - NIL. Firing as per appendix No 11. Men carried 9000 rounds of S.A.A. to No 15 position and sandbags were drawn from Dump. The work at No 10 position was continued. Inspection of Guns, Arms, Emplacements and Dugouts. Nos 3 & 4 Sections were working all day at TOURNAY CAMP under C.R.E. Weather dull & cloudy.	
	Dec 12		Enemy shelled Section HQ with 5.9 at 2 AM - 10 shells. OAF AVENUE with .77. Working party seen moving up at 2pm. At 4.45 pm RAILWAY TRENCH by OAF AVENUE was shelled. Machine Gun fire was hitting No 16 position from the direction of GAME COPSE or MAY FARM. Casualties - NIL. Firing as per appendix No 12.	

WAR DIARY
or
INTELLIGENCE SUMMARY.
(Erase heading not required.)

Instructions regarding War Diaries and Intelligence Summaries are contained in F. S. Regs., Par. II. and the Staff Manual respectively. Title pages will be prepared in manuscript.

Army Form C. 2118.

Place	Date	Hour	Summary of Events and Information	Remarks and references to Appendices
	1917			
	Dec 12	(cont.)	The weather was poor with a light mist all day.	
			The Sections out of the line were on working party under C.R.E at	
			TOURNAY CAMP as on the previous day.	
	Dec 13		OAF AVENUE, RAILWAY EMBANKMENT, + FUSILIER WOOD were fired on	
			during the day by the enemy. Nos 9 + 10 positions reported a good	
			deal of shelling round that area with 5.9 Enemy M.G sniping	
			on RAILWAY EMBANKMENT at 5 p.m.	
			Casualties — Nil. Firing as per appendix No 13.	
			Sections had a general cleaning up and No 6 Emplacement on	
			the side of RAILWAY EMBANKMENT was camouflaged.	
			Inspections were carried out as per routine.	
			Half Company out of the line engaged at TOURNAY CAMP on working	
			party. Very dull with some rain.	

A6945 Wt. W11422/M1160 350,000 12/16 D. D. & L. Forms/C./2118/14.

WAR DIARY or INTELLIGENCE SUMMARY

Army Form C. 2118.

(Erase heading not required.)

Place	Date	Hour	Summary of Events and Information	Remarks and references to Appendices
	1917 Dec 14		Enemy fired on OAK AVENUE, RAILWAY EMBANKMENT, FUSILIER WOOD, and to right of JARROCKS FARM with 5.9, 4.2. Otherwise there was nothing special to report from the line. 1 Sick. Weather fair. Firing as per appendix No. 14. Emplacement for No 6 Gun was built up. All guns of No 1 Section were re-laid. 6000 SAA carried to No 9 Position. S.O.S. line altered at all positions. The usual inspections of Guns, Arms etc were carried out. Sections out of the line engaged on working party at TOURNAY CAMP.	
	Dec 15		Enemy artillery was quiet all day. M.G. sniped Nos 7 & 8 Guns with explosive bullets. Casualties - NIL. Firing as per appendix No 15. A new fire screen was made for No 9 Gun. No 5 pumping as usual. Examination of Belts and Spareparts. Nos 7 & 8 Emplacements were improved. Nos 3 & 4 Sections relieved 1 & 2 in the line. Weather was fine.	

WAR DIARY
or
INTELLIGENCE SUMMARY.
(*Erase heading not required.*)

Army Form C. 2118.

Instructions regarding War Diaries and Intelligence Summaries are contained in F. S. Regs., Part II. and the Staff Manual respectively. Title pages will be prepared in manuscript.

Place	Date	Hour	Summary of Events and Information	Remarks and references to Appendices
	1917 Dec 16		Enemy fired on OAF AVENUE, + IMPERIAL AVENUE and shelled no 2 Section Headquarters at 4.40pm with 4.5's - 11 shells. Nos 9 + 10 Guns were fired at from 11.35pm to midnight — 40 shells. He also shelled RAVINE, OAF AVENUE, + IMPERIAL AVENUE with a few small shells. Enemy's MGs were also very busy. Casualties - Nil. Weather fine - misty. The men in the line were working on the emplacements, pumping etc. A pit was dug at no 7. 6000 SAA carried, and all tins were collected and properly buried. Empty cartridge cases were salvaged. Lt. Faulkner visited the Right and Left Centre Batts 119th during the night. Sections out of the line were employed on working party. The RNAI CAMP as before.	
	Dec 17		A quiet day in the line. Enemy MG was sniping at nos 7 + 8 Guns otherwise there was nothing to report. Casualties — NIL Firing as per appendix no 16. Weather — good. A new fire screen was made for no 9 Gun and inspection	

A6945 Wt. W11422/M1160 350,000 12/16 D. D. & L. Forms/C./2118/14.

WAR DIARY
or
INTELLIGENCE SUMMARY.
(Erase heading not required.)

Army Form C. 2118.

Place	Date	Hour	Summary of Events and Information	Remarks and references to Appendices
	1917 Dec 17 (cont'd)		were carried out as per routine. The two sections in camp were employed as a working party at TOURNAY CAMP as before.	
	Dec 18		Enemy artillery quiet again to-day, but they fired M.G's continuously throughout the night. Casualties - NIL Firing as per appendix No 17. Weather Good & clear The Duckboard track to RAILWAY TRENCH was improved and Salvage carried to TRANSPORT CORNER. A general clean up of dugouts, trench and Gun positions, and all rubbish was properly buried. Inspections of Respirators, arms, Guns & ammunition. Sections in camp employed as working party as above.	
	Dec 19		During the night 18/19th enemy searched along the embankment with light calibre shells evidently trying for our T.M.B. Guns. Nos 9, 15 & 16 Gun positions were shelled with 4.2 and 5.9, the CLUSTERS at 6.45 AM and Section	

WAR DIARY or INTELLIGENCE SUMMARY

Army Form C. 2118.

Place	Date	Hour	Summary of Events and Information	Remarks and references to Appendices
Richebourg	1917		Headquarters at night.	
			Casualties - Nil. Weather fine. Temp as per appendix No 18. Ammunition was hurried. No 5 gun firing II Trench Bombs carried from R.E. Dump to Section H.Q. and Boot musk to RAILWAY TRENCH. Salvage - Empty cases carried to dump, to be had on our limber.	
		11.20	Artillery on both sides was very active to-day, most of our fire being directed on the enemy dump. The Battalion & Brigade positions were heavily shelled with various shells of minenwerfer, Hi-Ex and Gas Shells were used on the 18 Gun which necessitated the use of gas masks. There were no casualties. Enemy MG's fired on the dug-out and also IMPERIAL AVENUE during the afternoon. No 19. Weather fine, mostly in morning. 5000 S.A.A. carried to the 15 position. Anti-Aircraft emplacement made at No 15 position. New Front position made for No 9. Sniping position started in trench. Guns were cleaned and ammunition turned and Salvage carried to limber.	

A6945 Wt. W11422/M1160 350,000 12/16 D.D.&L. Forms/C./2118/14.

WAR DIARY
or
INTELLIGENCE SUMMARY.

(Erase heading not required.)

Army Form C. 2118.

Place	Date	Hour	Summary of Events and Information	Remarks and references to Appendices
	1917 Dec 20 (contd)		Two sections out of the line were engaged on working party under C.R.E. at TOURNAY CAMP.	
	Dec 21		Enemy shelled Section H.Q. + IMPERIAL TRENCH near S.H.Q. from 5.45 p.m. to 5.45 A.m, also around nos 15 + 16 positions during the same time. Lt Faulkner visited right and left centre Battn Hqrs. Casualties – NIL – firing as per appendix no. 20. Weather was good – frosty. Inspections carried out as per routine. All guns and Gun kit thoroughly cleaned up and work continued on Sniping emplacement. Salvage carried on. Sections out of the line still employed at TOURNAY CAMP daily. 2nd Lt Oliver proceeded on leave, and Sergt F Ryrie to UK for commission.	
	Dec 22		Enemy was fairly active all night and sent over about 80 Gas shells into BATTLEWOOD between 4.30 + 6.30 A.m. and kept up sniping with MG's. Casualties – NIL Firing as per appendix no 21. Weather fine + very cold. nos 1 + 2 Sections relieved nos 3 + 4	

WAR DIARY
or
INTELLIGENCE SUMMARY

Army Form C. 2118.

Place	Date	Hour	Summary of Events and Information	Remarks and references to Appendices
	1917			
	Dec 22		in the line. 2nd Lt Inverson relieved Lt Carter M.C. at SPOILBANK. Morning of fine. There were important after noon	
	Dec 23		Enemy shelled RAVINE near 15.16 positions and OAF AVENUE at 4.30 the 15 - 4.30 fm. He took cover from S.H.Q. to RAILWAY TRENCH was also shelled. Casualties - Nil. Owing to the appendix No 22. 60000 S.A.A. was carried during the course of the day and ammunition found of all positions. No 3rd Section on working party - TOURNAY CAMP. Weather fine.	Appx 22
			Rather a quiet day in the line and there was nothing to report. Enemy artillery turned up during the night. 2nd Lt Thornton was gassed.	
	Dec 24		Very cold + frosty. Owing as per appendix No. 23 ammunition was carried to Gun positions + the minor inspections were carried out. Section on of the line on working party - TOURNAY CAMP. 2nd Lt Weston returned from leave.	Appx 23

A6945 Wt.W1142/M1160 350,000 12/16 D.D.&L. Forms/C/2118/14.

WAR DIARY
or
INTELLIGENCE SUMMARY.
(Erase heading not required.)

Army Form C. 2118.

Instructions regarding War Diaries and Intelligence Summaries are contained in F. S. Regs., Part II. and the Staff Manual respectively. Title pages will be prepared in manuscript.

Place	Date	Hour	Summary of Events and Information	Remarks and references to Appendices
	1917 Dec 25		Xmas day. Enemy were active at 7.45 AM about 30 shells 5.9 were dropped round IMPERIAL DUGOUTS & the RAILWAY EMBANKMENT. Our infantry "stood to" from 7.30 pm - 11 pm but nothing transpired and the night was exceptionally quiet. Casualties – NIL. Firing as per appendix no. 24. Gun emplacements were improved. The Sections out of the line did not go on the working party. 2nd Lt Weatherill proceeded to take charge of No 2 Section in the line, upon 2nd Lt Thornton being gassed. A concert was held in RIDGEWOOD CAMP in the evening, in which No 247 MG Coy joined, and a very pleasant evening was spent.	
	Dec 26		BATTLE WOOD & FUSILIER WOOD were shelled with shells of small calibre at intervals. 1 Casualty – Pte Linton – Wounded. Sections in camp on working party TOURNAY CAMP. Very cold and snowing. Firing as per appendix no 25	

WAR DIARY
or
INTELLIGENCE SUMMARY.
(*Erase heading not required.*)

Army Form C. 2118.

Instructions regarding War Diaries and Intelligence Summaries are contained in F. S. Regs., Part II. and the Staff Manual respectively. Title pages will be prepared in manuscript.

Place	Date	Hour	Summary of Events and Information	Remarks and references to Appendices
	1917			
	Dec 27		BATTLE WOOD, FUSILIER WOOD, & JARROCKS FARM were shelled with Gas shells, also hos 7 & 8 Gun positions. No 1 Section HQ was shelled in the morning with 5.9 & Gas shells. Casualties – NIL – Weather Good, very cold. Firing as per appendix ho 26 SAA was carried to hos 15 & 16 Guns. Working party at TOURNAY CAMP was recalled about noon and the Company moved to BAROSSA CAMP. Move was completed about 6 pm.	
	Dec 28		A quiet day in the line, and nothing much to report with the exception of a few shells of small calibre falling around TRANSPORT CORNER. One or two also fell near 15 & 16 Gun positions. Firing as per appendix ho. 27 Casualties – NIL. Weather fair. Inspection of Box Respirators, arms etc was carried out.	

A6945 Wt. W11422/M1160 350,000 12/16 D. D. & L. Forms/C./2118/14.

WAR DIARY or INTELLIGENCE SUMMARY

Army Form C. 2118.

Place	Date	Hour	Summary of Events and Information	Remarks and references to Appendices
	1917 Dec 29		Enemy shelling same positions again to-day — TRANSPORT CORNER and hos 15 + 16 Gun positions. OAF AVENUE also came in for some slight attention. 1 Sick — Pte Gooch. Weather Fair. Firing as per appendix No 28. The usual inspections were carried out. 63rd Inf Bde was relieved by 112th. 10000 S.A.A. carried to positions during the day.	

63rd Brigade,
37th Division.

63rd MACHINE GUN COMPANY.

JANUARY 1918

FIRING REPORT   63rd M.G. Coy

TIME	GUN	POSITION	TARGETS	ROUNDS	REMARKS
8/1/18					
2/1/18	6		ZANDVOORDE	3000	
3/1/18	9		Pic 14 to	4150	
5/1/18	15 } 16		Pill d Central	4350	

Total 12020

3/1/18

63rd M.G. Coy

FIRING REPORT 63rd M.G. Coy.

TIME	GUN No.	POSITION	TARGETS	ROUNDS	REMARKS
1/2/18	15		P.I.C Trench	5500	
	16		CHATEAU FM	5000	
				10500	

2/1/18.

63rd M.G. Coy.

FIRING REPORT 63rd M.G. Coy

TIME	GUN NO	POSITION	TARGETS	ROUNDS	REMARKS
2/3	9		ZANDVOORDE	1250	
1/8	15		P.7.C Tracks	3000	
	16			3000	
				7250	

3/11/18

63rd M.G. Coy.

4

FIRING REPORT   63rd M.C.Coy.

TIME	GUN NO	POSITION	TARGETS	ROUNDS	REMARKS.
3/4	15	}	P.q.c.Track	4000	
1/18	16			3500	
				7500	

A/1/18   63rd M.C.Coy

Firing Report

63rd M.G. Coy

Time	Gun No	Position	Targets	Rounds	Remarks
4/5	15		Pic Tnode	2000	
1/8	16			2500	
				4500	

5/1/18

63rd M.G. Coy

63rd M G Coy

FIRING REPORT

TIME	GUN NO	POSITION	TARGETS	ROUNDS	REMARKS
5/6/18			NIL		
1/18					

6/1/18

63rd M. G. Coy.

FIRING REPORT

63rd M G Coy

TIME	GUN NO	POSITION	TARGETS	ROUNDS	REMARKS
6/7	9		ALASKA Hs	2000	
1/8	15			2000	Track near HOLLEBEKE
1/8	16			2500	Track from Lock 5
				6500	

4/1/18

63rd M G Coy.

8

63rd M.G Coy

FIRING REPORT

TIME	GUN·No	POSITION	TARGETS	ROUNDS	REMARKS
1/8	9		Zandvoorde	2000	
1/18	15		Road in P&A	2000	
	16		Tubex Rd.	2500	
				6500	

63rd M.G Coy.

8/1/18

Firing Report

63rd MG Coy

TIME	GUN NO	POSITION	TARGETS	ROUNDS	REMARKS
8/9	9		ZANDVOORDE	2000	Harassing
1/18	15		Rd nr P8a	2000	fire also kept
	16		TUBEX Ho	2000	up during
				6000	the night.

9/1/8

63rd MG Coy.

63rd M G Coy.

FIRING REPORT

TIME	GUN NO	POSITION	TARGETS	ROUNDS	REMARKS
9/10	15		Tubex RL	2000	
1/18	16		Do	2000	
				4000	

10/1/18

63rd M G Coy.

FIRING REPORT

63rd M G Coy

TIME	GUN NO	POSITION	TARGETS	ROUNDS	REMARKS
10/11	15		Trench	2000	
11/8	16		P 7 a	2000	
				4000	

11/11/18

63rd M G Coy.

WAR DIARY
or
INTELLIGENCE SUMMARY

Army Form C. 2118.

63RD MACHINE GUN COMPANY.

Place	Date	Hour	Summary of Events and Information	Remarks and references to Appendices
BATTLE WOOD	June 1918		TRANSPORT CORNER were shelled by the enemy at odd intervals during the morning. 4 Shells per annum No 10 Gun during this time and RAILWAY TRENCH was shelled with light calibre shells. There are casualties. The weather was lovely good. Subbing positions at 1.30 & at 5.55 am finished. A spare supernumerary was started at No 9 Gun. No 5 Gun early having as warned the chests at Bois Cornador and informing the chief the enemy salvage was carried to finders. Officer the last four impressions of Bois Cornador. During as per appendix No. 1			
	June 2		The Enemy put Gas Shells on & along IMPERIAL AVENUE and all four teams at two Bastiage in camp area on a selvance front. 15 pm to 11 pm except No it had to move there (See Explanation) between 6.14 pm & about 15.16 B. Bastiage and BATTLE WOOD hardly shelled. The line behind CAF AVENUE was also shelled and gas shell. 2 hour reported sick. Weather fine. During the day 1000 S.A.A. was carried up as per appendix No 2. During the day 1000 S.A.A. was carried up to No 16 Gun and dugouts were thoroughly cleared also Gun side after.	

19/6/18

MM2

WAR DIARY or INTELLIGENCE SUMMARY.

(Erase heading not required.)

Army Form C. 2118.

Place	Date	Hour	Summary of Events and Information	Remarks and references to Appendices
LINE	1918 Jan 2 (contd)		etc. and the usual inspections of arms etc took place. The men in Camp were inspected by the C.O.	
	Jan 3		BATTLE WOOD & TRANSPORT CORNER were shelled intermittently throughout the day and night. About 12 Gas shells fell in BATTLE WOOD near No 16 Gun at 2 A.M. Section H.Q. was also shelled at odd intervals. Casualties - Nil. Weather Good. Firing as per appendix No 3. 30.000 Rounds S.A.A. was carried to Section H.Q. and salvage carried to limbers. Work was continued on sniping emplacement. All Guns Rifles, Revolvers and ammunition was cleaned. A cross was erected over the grave of Private Ryan 58th M.G.Coy. The Half Company out of the line was on working party at RIDGEWOOD CAMP. 2nd Lt Forrest being in charge.	
	Jan 4		FUSILIER & BATTLE WOODS were shelled from the East during the night 4/5th some of the shells being Gas. Casualties - Nil. Weather Good after a very misty morning. Firing as per Appendix No 4. Very little work done owing to relief. Nos 1 & 2 Sections relieved	

WAR DIARY
or
INTELLIGENCE SUMMARY
(Erase heading not required.)

Army Form C. 2118.

Place	Date	Hour	Summary of Events and Information	Remarks and references to Appendices
LINE	1918 June 3rd		(contd) in the line. Relieved BAROSSA CAMP at 1.30 pm to entrain at KILMARNOCK SIDING at 2 pm.	
	June 5		Rather a quiet day on the line but for a few shells dropping in FUSILIER WOODS (site of smoke candle). Men in working parties. Casualties — Nil. Weather fine. Firing as per Appendix No 5	
	June 6		Our own artillery in this sector were very active all day and the enemy in retaliation shelled IMPERIAL AVENUE BATTLE WOOD and FUSILIER WOOD at intervals during the day and night. Some gas were inhaled. [illeg] received last night (5th). A good rest day. Casualties — Nil. Firing as per Appendix No 6. Salvage was collected and carried to Limbers. No 3 Section (One of the line) centralised limbs and gear etc when No 2 Section attended Church Parade.	

WAR DIARY
or
INTELLIGENCE SUMMARY.
(Erase heading not required.)

Army Form C. 2118.

Instructions regarding War Diaries and Intelligence Summaries are contained in F. S. Regs., Part II. and the Staff Manual respectively. Title pages will be prepared in manuscript.

Place	Date	Hour	Summary of Events and Information	Remarks and references to Appendices
LINE	1918 Jan 7		Intermittent shelling of our area all day by the Enemy, and during the night - very quiet. All ammunition turned, and at No 5 Position - pumping. Inspection of Box Respirators, Guns, Rifles etc. Good weather, but very poor visibility. Casualties - Nil. Firing as per Appendix No 7. Sections out of the line were employed on miscellaneous fatigues in Camp.	
	Jan 8		Enemy fired a quantity of shells during the day (150) into the South end of BATTLE WOOD and FUSILIER WOOD and area. One of his machine Guns was very troublesome traversing along trench S.E of THE CLUSTERS. 12 light Calibre shells fell in RAILWAY TRENCH and around No 1 Section H.Q. 2nd Lt Weatherill was gassed. The Weather was fine, but a heavy mist most of the day which made observation difficult. Firing as per Appendix No 8. Five teams under 2nd Lt Faulkner left Camp for the line at 12.30pm to take up special positions for Raid. The positions were previously	

WAR DIARY
or
INTELLIGENCE SUMMARY.
(Erase heading not required.)

Army Form C. 2118.

Instructions regarding War Diaries and Intelligence Summaries are contained in F. S. Regs., Part. II. and the Staff Manual respectively. Title pages will be prepared in manuscript.

Place	Date	Hour	Summary of Events and Information	Remarks and references to Appendices
LINE	1918 Jan 8 (cont'd)		reconnoitred by 2nd Lt Laughton + 2nd Lt Faulkner on Sunday January 6th 1918.	
	Jan 9		A very quiet day on the whole, what few shells came over were sent at long intervals and no casualties resulted. 2nd Lt Weatherill went down the line as result of being gassed yesterday. General cleaning up and the usual inspections. The day was fairly clear. The remaining men in Camp were cleaning Huts etc. Firing as per Appendix No 9	
	Jan 10		Enemy was very active during the night but not around our positions. M G active at GAME COPSE The Ground was frozen and covered in snow. The trenches were good but the duckboards very slippery. On our left and right a raid was carried out at 12.30 A.m by our troops. General cleaning up and the usual inspections took place. Casualties – Nil. Firing as per Appendix No 10 2nd Lt Faulkner and teams arrived in Camp during the afternoon. Transport left for new area.	

A6945 Wt. W11422/M1160 350,000 12/16 D. D. & L. Forms/C./2118/14.

WAR DIARY
or
INTELLIGENCE SUMMARY.

(Erase heading not required.)

Army Form C. 2118.

Instructions regarding War Diaries and Intelligence Summaries are contained in F. S. Regs., Part II. and the Staff Manual respectively. Title pages will be prepared in manuscript.

Place	Date	Hour	Summary of Events and Information	Remarks and references to Appendices
LINE	1918 Jan 11		A very quiet day after the Raid and little to report. General cleaning up before relief and inspection of Box Respirators, Rifles etc. Casualties - Nil. Firing as per Appendix No 11. The Weather was good. Nos 3 & 4 Sections went into the line and Guns were overhauled.	
T 27 sheet 27 SW	Jan 12		Company entrained at DICKEBUSCH at 10 AM for new training area. Detrained at EBBLINGHEM about 2 pm. Arrived in Billets about 3 pm. The Transport already arrived. Billets very widely scattered.	
	Jan 13		Company Resting.	
	Jan 14		Kit inspection for the Company. Cleaning up and inspection by O.C. Company.	
	Jan 15		A programme of training for the week was drawn up. The day's work consisted of - Infantry and Saluting drill, Mechanism and I.A., Lock stripping etc, and a lecture on Map Reading. Weather fair.	

WAR DIARY
or
INTELLIGENCE SUMMARY.
(Erase heading not required.)

Army Form C. 2118.

Instructions regarding War Diaries and Intelligence Summaries are contained in F. S. Regs., Par. II. and the Staff Manual respectively. Title pages will be prepared in manuscript.

Place	Date	Hour	Summary of Events and Information	Remarks and references to Appendices
T 27 Sheet 27 SW	1917 Jan 16		Training programme continued. A route march was included in the mornings work. Weather fair.	
	Jan 17		Infantry Drill. Revolver Drill Gun Drill, and Elementary Training mechanism and I A. In the afternoon. Recreation. Football. Weather continues fair.	
	Jan 18		Training programme continued. Checking of all mobilisation kit by D.A.D.O.S	
	Jan 19		Lecture on overhead fire and a route march which lasted all the morning. The afternoon was spent in recreation. Football matches between the Sections, and in the evening the Company had their annual Xmas dinner, which was a great success and enjoyed by everyone.	
	Jan 20		Sunday. The Company rested.	
	Jan 21		The Company had Baths at BLAIRINGHEM. Nos 1 and 2 Sections were on the Range. Weather fine.	

A6945 Wt. W11422/M1160 350,000 12/16 D. D. & L. Forms/C./2118/14.

WAR DIARY or INTELLIGENCE SUMMARY.

(Erase heading not required.)

Army Form C. 2118.

Place	Date	Hour	Summary of Events and Information	Remarks and references to Appendices
T.27 Sheet 27 S.W.	1918 Jan 22		8.45 AM Inspection by O.C. Company. The Sections were on a small scheme together. Nos 1 + 2 Sections under Lt Thomson, Nos 3 + 4 under 2nd Lt Laughton. Cleaning up preparatory to inspection by Divisional General.	
	Jan 23		The Company was inspected by G.O.C. 37th Division. Football in the afternoon.	
U.20.A.	Jan 24		The Company moved into new Billets at N 21 a (Sheet 27 S.W.), leaving old Billets at 10.30 AM and arriving in the new area 11.45 AM. Weather fine.	
	Jan 25		The Week's programme was continued — Infantry Arms Drill, Lecture on the Compass, Mechanism + I.A. and Revolver Drill. Weather fine again.	
	Jan 26		The Sections were at the disposal of C.S.M. Buchanan of the Army Gymnastic Staff for one hour each Physical Training. Remainder of morning was spent in cleaning Gun Kit etc. Football match in the afternoon. Fine all day.	

WAR DIARY
or
INTELLIGENCE SUMMARY.
(Erase heading not required.)

Instructions regarding War Diaries and Intelligence Summaries are contained in F. S. Regs., Par. II. and the Staff Manual respectively. Title pages will be prepared in manuscript.

Army. Form C. 2118.

Place	Date	Hour	Summary of Events and Information	Remarks and references to Appendices
U 20·a	1918 Jan 27		Church Parades for the Company in the morning	
			Iron Rations were turned over.	
			Fine Weather but very cold.	
	Jan 28		Training programme continued, the morning's work consisted	
			of Physical Training, Infantry Drill, a Lecture. Gun and	
			Revolver Drill. Football in the afternoon – Sectional matches	
			Fine and cold again.	
	Jan 29		The Company was inspected by C O and then Sections 2. 3. +4	
			went on Route March, whilst No 1 Section carried out a	
			Tactical Scheme. Very cold all day.	
	Jan 30		The Whole Company carried out a Tactical Scheme from 9 a.m.	
			until 1 pm 1·2 Sections with the Guns whilst the remaining	
			sections acted as a body of Infantry.	
			The afternoon was spent in football. Very cold again.	

A6945 Wt. W11422/M1160 350,000 12/16 D. D. & L. Forms/C./2118/14.

WAR DIARY or INTELLIGENCE SUMMARY.

Army Form C. 2118.

Place	Date	Hour	Summary of Events and Information	Remarks and references to Appendices
U.20.a	1918 Jan 31		Training programme - Physical Training, Infantry & Arms Drill mechanism and Stoppages, Lecture on Range Cards and Revolver drill during the morning. Further sectional football matches in the afternoon. A very sharp frost all day & very cold.	

for Commanding No. 63 Coy.
Machine Gun Corps.

Programme of Work 21/1/18 - 26/1/18

DATE	TIME	UNIT	DESCRIPTION OF TRAINING	LOCALITY	REMARKS
Jan 21'18	9 AM - 11	63rd M G Coy	BATHS		
	11 AM - 1 PM		No 1+2 Section - Range		
	11 - 12 NOON		Gun Drill		
	12 - 1 PM		Lecture Drill		
Jan 22nd'18	MORNING		TACTICAL SCHEME		
	AFTERNOON		Recreational Training		
Jan 23'18	9 - 10 AM		Infantry Section Drill		
	10 - 11 AM		Lecture - Principles For		
	11 - 12 NOON		Instruction - Recognition of Targets		
	12 - 1 PM		Inspection of arms kits of Section officers		
	Afternoon		Recreational Training		
Jan 24'18	9 - 10 AM		Infantry Drill		
	10 - 11		Lecture - The Compass		
	11 - 12 NOON		Musketry - I.A. Faults before, during & after firing		
	12 - 1 PM		Revolver Drill and Shoot Fast on Board		
	Afternoon		Recreational Training		
Jan 25'18	9 - 10 AM		TACTICAL SCHEME		
	MORNING				
	AFTERNOON		Recreational Training		
Jan 26'18	9 - 10 AM		Lecture - Map Reading		
	10 - 1 PM		Company Route March (Recreational Training)		
	Afternoon				

Programme of Work.

DATE	TIME	UNIT	DESCRIPTION OF TRAINING	LOCALITY	REMARKS
Jan 21st 1918	9 AM to 11 AM	68th M.G. Coy	Cleaning of all Guns, Gun kit &c		
	11 - 12.30	"	Kit inspection and cleaning up of men's equipment		
	12.40	"	Inspection of Coy (Coy Transport) by O.C. Coy. Dress - Drill order.		
	Afternoon	"	Recreational Training		
Jan 22nd 18	9 AM to 10 AM	"	Infantry Drill + Saluting Drill		
	10 - 11 AM	"	Mechanism + I.A. Points before, during & after firing		
	11 - 12	"	Stripping of Lock. Blindfolded, taking of time		
	12 - 1 pm	"	Lecture - Map Reading & Compasses &c		
	Afternoon	"	Recreational Training		
Jan 23rd 18	9 - 10 AM	"	Infantry Drill		
	10 - 1 pm	"	Company Route March - Dress Fighting order		
	Afternoon	"	Recreational Training		
Jan 24 18	9 - 10 AM	"	Infantry Drill		
		"	Revolver Drill + Short lesson on ??		
		"	Gun Drill. Elementary Training		
		"	Mechanism + I.A.		
		"	Recreational Training		
Jan 25 18	9 - 10 AM	"	Infantry Drill		
		"	Mechanism I.A. Points before, during, after firing		
		"	?? Elementary Training		
		"	Lecture - ??		
		"	??		
		"	Recreational Training		
		"	?? Sion fighting ??		

DATE	TIME	UNIT	DESCRIPTION OF TRAINING	LOCALITY	REMARKS
1917					
Jan 28	8.30-9.30	68th M Coy	Physical Training		
	9.30-10	"	Infantry Drill, Arms Drill		
	10-11	"	Lecture (Execution of duties)		
	11-12	"	Gun Drill		
	12-1pm	"	Revolver Drill		
Jan 29	9.00-9.30	"	C.O. Inspection		
	9.30-12	"	ROUTE MARCH		
Jan 30	8.30-9.30	"	Physical Training		
	9.30-10	"	Infantry Drill, Arms Drill, Saluting		
	10-12	"	TACTICAL SCHEME. (action from billets on given fronts)		
Jan 31	8.45-9.30	"	Physical Training		
	9-10	"	Infantry Drill, Arms Drill		
	10-11	"	Intercommunication and stoppages		
	11-12	"	Lecture (Range cards)		
	12-1	"	Revolver Practice		
Feb 1	9.00-9.30	"	C.O. Inspection		
	9.30-12	"	ROUTE MARCH		
Feb 2	8.30-9.30	"	Physical Training		
	9.30-10	"	Infantry Arms Drill, Saluting		
	10-12	"	TACTICAL SCHEME		
	12-1	"	Kit Inspection		
	1-2	"	the afternoon will be spent in Recreative Training		

1917 men at work for week ending February 2nd 1917

63rd Brigade.
37th Division.

Became part of 37th Battalion M.G.C. in March.

63rd MACHINE GUN COMPANY.

FEBRUARY 1918

WAR DIARY
or
INTELLIGENCE SUMMARY
(Erase heading not required.)

Army Form C. 2118

63RD COMPANY, MACHINE GUN CORPS

Place	Date	Hour	Summary of Events and Information	Remarks and references to Appendices
U21a	1918 July 1st		The Company was paraded at 9 a.m. for observation of conduct sheets. Afterwards scheme but owing to Rough weather the Scheme was put off and ordinary training was carried out instead in the afternoon.	
	July 2		The company carried on the daily training as per programme. 2 NCOs Sergeants Roberts & Evans attended a gas lecture at Headquarters 10th New Lancaster. Weather very rough wet and cold.	
	July 3		No Sections were on the Range at T.28.d. Very rough and wet again.	
	July 4		No day training. Engineer Training (carried by C.O. Inspection) in full marching order at 9.30 am. from 10.15 AM en route march. Fair and some improvement made in fighting order.	

WAR DIARY
or
INTELLIGENCE SUMMARY.
(Erase heading not required.)

Army Form C.2...

Instructions regarding War Diaries and Intelligence Summaries are contained in F. S. Regs., Part II. and the Staff Manual respectively. Title pages will be prepared in manuscript.

Place	Date	Hour	Summary of Events and Information	Remarks and references to Appendices
U 21 a Sheet 27 SW	1918 Feb 5		CSM Buchanan of the Army Gymnastic Staff came to take the men in Physical Training first thing in the morning. This was followed by Training programme under Section Officers. Football matches in the afternoon. Weather fair.	Appendix 2
	Feb 6		The Company paraded at 9 am for Contact Aeroplane Scheme but owing to bad weather this was again put off, and the men carried out the programme of training for the day. Very rough weather.	
	Feb 7		Section Turnout competition was held under the Brigadier General 63rd Inf Brigade. In the afternoon we sent a team over to the Brigade ground to play the Semi final of the football competition but were beaten by the Middlesex. Very rough weather.	

WAR DIARY
or
INTELLIGENCE SUMMARY

Army Form C. 2118.

Place	Date	Hour	Summary of Events and Information	Remarks and references to Appendices
M310 Sheet 27 SW	1918 Jul 8		At 8.30 am the Company was inspected by the CO and then the training programme for the day was proceeded with - Infantry and Arms drill competition. At 10 o'clock the Company was inspected by Lieut Weston 250 Coy reminders were examined later. Weather was fine.	Appendix 2
	Jul 9		The morning was spent in marching to a given point by the purpose of telephone elevation but the scheme was cancelled owing to rough weather and the company returned to lines.	
	Jul 10		Sunday - Opportunity was taken of using the Range and the company practised her 15 sections at intervals during the day.	Appendix 3
	Jul 11		The company assisted in the packing of Transport into fresh areas orders to move the following day to new area.	
	Jul 12		Transport left for new area. Weather fair.	

A6945 Wt.W1422/M1160 350,000 12/16 D.D.&L. Forms/C./2118/14.

WAR DIARY or INTELLIGENCE SUMMARY.

Army Form C. 2118

Place	Date	Hour	Summary of Events and Information	Remarks and references to Appendices
U 21 A Sheet 27 SW	1918 Feb 13		The Company less Transport entrained at EBBLINGHEM for ABEELE and arrived at CHIPPAWA CAMP at 8 p.m. It was a very wet journey and on arrival at HAZEBROUCK the Company was billeted for three hours until able to proceed by train.	

WAR DIARY
or
INTELLIGENCE SUMMARY.
(*Erase heading not required.*)

Instructions regarding War Diaries and Intelligence Summaries are contained in F. S. Regs., Part II. and the Staff Manual respectively. Title pages will be prepared in manuscript.

Army Form C. 2...

Place	Date	Hour	Summary of Events and Information	Remarks and references to Appendices
1918	1918			
LINE	Feb 14		Relieved the 61st M.G. Coy in the line. Relief complete 6 p.m.	
			A rather quiet night in the line. Our guns shelled tracks at J27 b,d	
			Enemy did little artillery work, putting 6 shells 4.2 into our positions	
			during the night. Casualties NIL. Firing as per appendix no. —	
			Nos 3 & 4 Sections went into the line first, leaving Camp at 1 pm	
			and entraining at DICKEBUSCH	
	Feb 15		Our guns (MG's) were busy firing on FAIR COTTS (J28 a 56 42) and MENIN ROAD	
			(J22 d 00 28) whilst Enemy retaliated by sweeping our nos 2 + 3 positions	
			Artillery quiet in our Sector. Casualties NIL. Firing as per appendix no —	
			The weather was good and frosty.	
	Feb 16		Our MGs fired on SWAGGER FARM and junction of duckboards at J27 d 50 45	
			but beyond this there was little activity. Casualties NIL —	
			Firing as per appendix no. 4 — The weather good and frosty again.	
			Nos 1 + 2 Sections proceeded to TORR TOP TUNNELS in reserve.	

A6945 Wt. W11422/M1160 350,000 12/16 D. D. & L. Forms/C./2118/14.

WAR DIARY
or
INTELLIGENCE SUMMARY.
(Erase heading not required.)

Army Form C. 2118

Place	Date	Hour	Summary of Events and Information	Remarks and references to Appendices
LINE	1918 Feb 17		In the early morning our artillery were firing a little. The enemy put a few shells near our Nos 2, 3 & 4 Guns (J.25.b 29.82), and their machine guns were active at night. The weather being very cold, our guns fired only to keep warm. Great activity in the air today. Casualties Nil. Firing as per appendix No 5	
	Feb 18		A quiet day on the whole a few shells being dropped in J.25.a in the evening, but no casualties resulted. Machine Guns were busy throughout the day. Enemy Aircraft in our sector was engaged by AA guns. Casualties Nil. Firing as per appendix No 6	
	Feb 19		Enemy shelled our back areas with a few gas shells during the day and we retaliated by shelling the HOLLEBEKE sector. Our MG's fired on FAIR COTTS & X Roads J22.35.60. Casualties Nil. Firing as per appendix No 7	

WAR DIARY
or
INTELLIGENCE SUMMARY.
(Erase heading not required.)

Instructions regarding War Diaries and Intelligence Summaries are contained in F. S. Regs., Part II. and the Staff Manual respectively. Title pages will be prepared in manuscript.

Army Form C. 21

Place	Date	Hour	Summary of Events and Information	Remarks and references to Appendices
LINE	1918 Feb 19		(Cont'd) Weather. Good & frosty.	
	Feb 20		Enemy heavy battery engaged our 18 pounders just north of the MENIN ROAD at 4 o'clock in the morning, and in the evening put about 20 round on J 25. Our artillery was active all day. Enemy MG's fired on us from direction LEWIS HO - BERRY COTTS. Casualties Nil. Weather very poor. Firing as per appendix no 8	
	Feb 21		A good deal of activity was displayed on both sides today. Enemy artillery fired on J 25 central, STOUT TRACK and track running through BODMIN COPSE, the shooting being directed by aeroplane. Machine Guns fired on our nos 5 & 6 positions but no casualties resulted. A shelter was made for ammunition at no 7 Gun and a general cleaning up of dugout etc. Inspections as per routine. Weather Visibility very good Firing as per appendix no 9	

A6945 Wt. W11422/M1160 350,000 12/16 D. D. & L. Forms/C./2118/14.

WAR DIARY or INTELLIGENCE SUMMARY.

Army Form C. 2118.

Instructions regarding War Diaries and Intelligence Summaries are contained in F. S. Regs., Part II. and the Staff Manual respectively. Title pages will be prepared in manuscript.

(Erase heading not required.)

Place	Date	Hour	Summary of Events and Information	Remarks and references to Appendices
LINE	1918 Feb 22		Section relief last night. Complete 6.10 pm. A quiet day in the line. Only a few shells were dropped between 9.25 pm and 10 pm. otherwise there is little to report. Casualties - Nil. Firing as per appendix no. 10 Weather fair.	
	Feb 23		Our artillery was firing on enemy front & support lines throughout the day whilst a good deal of black shrapnel was put over by him by our Section HQrs. Our no 5 & 6 positions were swept by his machine guns. The Sections out of the line stationed in TORR TOP TUNNELS - were on carrying parties and also provide piquets and patrols for the Tunnels. Sgt Hunt reported sick to day. No casualties. Inspection of Box respirators, rifles revolvers etc. Weather fairly good Firing as per appendix no 11	
	Feb 24		Active on both sides. Our nos 5 & 6 positions were shelled by the enemy with 4.2's at intervals. Gas shells were also dropped about J.25.b.05 between 6-7 pm. A few fell near Section HQ. Enemy MG's fired on tracks through DUMBARTON WOOD. A lot of work was got through by the men in the line, belt filling, and an emplacement built at S.H.Q. Casualties Nil. Firing as per appendix no 12.	

WAR DIARY
or
INTELLIGENCE SUMMARY

Army Form C. 2118.

Place	Date	Hour	Summary of Events and Information	Remarks and references to Appendices
LINE	1918 Jul 25		A few 4.2's were put over the back left of SHQ during the morning & very quiet the rest of the day. At midnight however enemy put over a great number of gas shells — mostly the gun positions also 12.30 am. He moved the firing to the left & far rear. From then he continued to shell gas areas at around our area till nearly 6 am. There was a great deal of shelling until he M4's around our front & SHQ. No casualties. N2. Weather extremely good.	
	Jul 26		We did a lot of firing to-day as per appendix No — Our artillery was very active on our left during the night & rather heavy was quiet until 11.30 am when he became active until 5.15 am. Mostly were in vicinity of J.25 & 30.85 and only shells in our own gun areas. Duplication of 130x natured. Gas, mortars etc. Casualties — Nil. Firing as per appendix No 14 Very good weather.	

WAR DIARY
or
INTELLIGENCE SUMMARY.
(Erase heading not required.)

Army Form C. 2118.

Instructions regarding War Diaries and Intelligence Summaries are contained in F. S. Regs., Part II. and the Staff Manual respectively. Title pages will be prepared in manuscript.

Place	Date	Hour	Summary of Events and Information	Remarks and references to Appendices
FRONT LINE	1918 Feb 27		Enemy very active again. At midnight over 100 heavy shells were thrown on back areas in rapid succession, close to Coy HQ. Our artillery put down a Barrage 4am to 5am. His MG Snipers were busy with short bursts. Casualties - Nil - Weather Good.	
	Feb 28		The usual activity with our own artillery and MGs. Enemy more active than usual by night. Round both guns (7 & 8) he put a good deal of 4·2's, and also tracks. His TMs were active on STEVENS TRENCH and round No 8 Gun. 50 shells were dropped around No 2 Sec HQ between 1 and 2 am. No Casualties resulted. An A A emplacement was built and about 20000 rounds SAA carried from Company HQ to No 2 Section HQ. Inspections as per routine. Firing as per appendix No. 15. Weather fairly good, but the condition of the ground is very bad.	

W.O.Chak 2/7/18

Commanding No. 63 Coy
Machine Gun Corps.

Appendix No 1

Copy: Scheme of work for week ending February 2nd 1908

DATE 1908	TIME	UNIT	DESCRIPTION OF TRAINING	LOCALITY	REMARKS
Jan 28	8.30-9.20	68th M.Coy	Physical Training		
	9.20-10	"	Infantry Drill + arms drill		
	10-11	"	Lecture - (succession of duties)		
	11-12	"	Gun Drill		
	12-1pm	"	Recreation drill		
Jan 29	8.20-9.20	"	C.O. Inspection		
		"	ROUTE MARCH		
Jan 30	8.50-9.30	"	Physical Training		
	9.30-10	"	Infantry Drill, arms drill + Saluting		
		"	TACTICAL SCHEME (action from limber on gun target)		
Jan 31	8.30-9.20	"	Physical Training		
	9.20-10	"	Infantry + arms drill		
	10-11	"	Intercommunication and stoppages		
	11-12	"	Lecture (Range Card)		
	12-1	"	Section Drill		
Feb 1	8.20-9.20	"	C.O. Inspection		
		"	ROUTE MARCH		
Feb 2	8.50-9.20	"	Physical Training		
	9.30-10	"	Infantry arms Drill, + Saluting		
	10-12	"	TACTICAL SCHEME		
	1-12	"	Kit Inspection		

The afternoons will be spent in Recreation training.

Programme of Work for men _____

Appendix 2

Date	Time	Unit	Description of Training		Remarks
1919 Feb 4th	8.50-9.20	63rd M.G. Coy	Physical Training		
	9.35-10	"	C.O. Inspection (Full marching order)		
	10.15	"	ROUTE MARCH (Fighting order)		
Feb 5th	8.50-9.20	"	Physical Training		
	9.30-10	"	Infantry Drill		
	10.15	"	TACTICAL SCHEME		
Feb 6th	8.50-9.20	"	Physical Training		
	9.30-10	"	Infantry Drill		
	10.15-10.45	"	Gas Drill		
	10.45-11.30	"	Gun Drill		
	11.30-1 pm	"	Revolver Drill		
Feb 7th	8.50-9.20	"	Physical Training		
	9.30-10	"	Infantry Drill		
	10.15	"	TACTICAL SCHEME		
Feb 8th	8.50-9.20	"	Physical Training		
	9.30-10.30	"	Infantry Drill		
	10.30-11.30	"	Mechanism & Stoppages		
	11.30-12.30	"	Lecture		
	12.30-1 pm	"	Gas Drill		
Feb 9th	8.50-9.20	"	Physical Training		
	9.30-	"	C.O. Inspection		
	10.15	"	ROUTE MARCH		

The afternoons will be spent in Recreational Training.

Programme of Work for week ending February 16th 1919   Appendix 3

DATE	TIME	UNIT	DESCRIPTION OF TRAINING	LOCALITY	REMARKS
February 11th	9¼-10 AM	63rd M.G.Coy	Physical Tng + Infantry Drill		
	10-10:30	"	Gas Drill		
	10:30-11:30	"	Combined Drill		
	11:30-12:30	"	Instruction - Recognition of Targets		3+4 Sections only
	12:30-1 pm	"	Sight setting and Aiming		
February 12	Afternoon	"	No 5 1+2 Section - Range Practice		
	9-10 AM	"	Physical Training + Infantry Drill		
	10-10:30	"	Lecture on Teamwork		
	10:30-11:30	"	Combined Drill		
	11:30-12:30	"	Instruction - Recognition of Targets		1+2 Sections only
	12:30-1 pm	"	Sight setting and Aiming		
February 13	Afternoon	"	No 6 3+4 Section - Range Practice		
	9-10 AM	"	Physical Training		
	10-10:30	"	Gas Drill		
	10:30-11	"	Lecture on Barrage		
	11-12	"	Barrage Drill		
	12-1 pm	"	stoppages		
February 14	9-10 AM	"	Physical Training + Infantry Drill		
	10-10:30	"	Lecture on "Anti-Gas Devices"		
	10:30-11:30	"	Barrage Drill		
	11:30-12	"	Indirect distance		
	12-1 pm	"	S.O.S. Drill		
February 15	9-10 AM	"	Physical Training + Infantry Drill		
	10-10:30	"	Gas Drill		
	10:30-11:30	"	stoppages		
	11:30-12	"	Lecture on "ammunition supplies" by Lieut Le Mesurier		
	12-1 pm	"	Combined Drill		
February 16	9-10 AM	"	Physical Training + Infantry Drill		
	10-10:30	"	Sight setting and aiming		
	10:30-11:30	"	Barrage Drill		
	11:30-12	"	Lecture on Camouflage by 2nd Lt R.A. Fountain		
	12-1 pm	"	gun bus with ammunition parks. Afternoon men to sports for recreation		

FIRING REPORT

TIME	GUN NO	TARGET	ROUNDS FIRED	REMARKS
	2	J27 d 80 45	2000	
16/17	5 & 6	SOS lines	1000	
	3	J27 b 30 35	2500	
	4	SOS lines	500	
		Total	6000	

16/2/18

63rd M C Coy

5

FIRING REPORT

TIME	GUN NO	TARGET	ROUNDS	REMARKS
17/18	1	} S.O Slures	2000	
	2			
	3			
	4			
	5			
	6			
		TOTAL	2000	

17/2/18

63rd M d Coy

FIRING REPORT

TIME	GUN NO	TARGET	ROUNDS	REMARKS
1510		J 21 d 50.40	500	
1610	1/6	J 71 6 70 30	2000	
	1/6	J 32 6 60 30	2000	
		J 32 c 60 60	2000	
		J 28 c 10 70	500	
		TOTAL	7000	

16/2/16

63rd M.G. Coy

6

FIRING REPORT

TIME	GUN NO	TARGET	ROUNDS	REMARKS
	1	J21 & 53 40	1000	
19/20	2	FAIR COTTS	3000	
	3	"	3000	
	4	X Roads J22 K56	3000	
	5	J28 c 20 70	500	
	6			
		TOTAL	10500	

19/7/18

63rd M.G. Coy

FIRING REPORT

TIME	GUN No	TARGET	ROUNDS	REMARKS
20/21	1/6	Thakoran	10750	320
		TOTAL	10750	

20/3/16

63rd M.G. Coy

9

FIRING REPORT

TIME	GUN-NO	TARGET	ROUNDS	REMARKS
21/22	1	GLASSHOUSES	3000	
	2	STONE FARM	3000	
	3	J22 c 80.35	3000	
	4	SWAGGER FARM	3250	
	5,6	J28 c 10.70	250	
		TOTAL	12,500	

21/2/18

63rd M G Coy

FIRING REPORT

TIME	GUN NO	TARGET	ROUNDS	REMARKS
22/23		COSY COTS		
	1/6		J22 c 30 20	
			J22 c 35 46	} 8500
			J22 c 30 65	
		TOTAL	8500	

22/7/18

63rd M.G. Coy

10

FIRING REPORT

TIME	GUN NO	TARGET	ROUNDS	REMARKS
	1	SWAGGER FARM	3000	
	2	ALASKA HOUSES	3500	
	3	J.12.c.5.4.	500	
	4	POT FARM	3000	
		TOTAL	10000	

23/9/18

63rd M.G. Coy

FIRING REPORT

TIME	GUN No	TARGET	ROUNDS	REMARKS
	1	J.22.c.20.30	3500	
24/6/5	2	THE MILL	4000	
	3	J.22.23.c.75	1500	GHELUVELT
	4	J.22.c.35.60	3500	
		TOTAL	12500	

24/9/17

63rd M.G. Coy

13

FIRING REPORT

TIME	GUN No	TARGET	ROUNDS	REMARKS
25/1/26	1	J28 a 30	2000	
	2	J22 c 80.40	4000	
	3	J22 c 50.60	3000	
	4	J27 b 15.70	3500	
		TOTAL	12500	

25/3/13

63rd M G Coy.

FIRING REPORT

TIME	GUN No	TARGET	ROUNDS	REMARKS
	1	T27 b.40.45	2000	
	2	T27 b.86.25	4000	
26/2	3	T27 b.45.55	3000	
	4	T26 b.12.70	2500	
	1	T21 c.50.35	1750	
	2	T31 c.30.20	2000	
	3	T32 c.35.46	1750	
	4	T32 c.30.65	1750	
		TOTAL	18750	

63rd MG Coy

FIRING REPORT

TIME	GUN NO	TARGET	ROUNDS	REMARKS
Feb 28	1/6	J22 35 60 to J22 70 30	8000	
		SOS lines	9000	
		TOTAL	17000	

26/2/18

63rd M G Coy